PASTA COOKBOOK

Myra Street

HAMLYN

London New York Sydney Toronto

CONTENTS

First published in 1974 by
THE HAMLYN PUBLISHING GROUP LIMITED
London · New York · Sydney · Toronto
Astronaut House, Feltham, Middlesex, England
© Copyright The Hamlyn Publishing Group Limited 1974
Second impression 1981

Trade edition ISBN 0 600 32292 0
Fiat edition ISBN 0 600 32293 9

Printed in Great Britain by
Fakenham Press Limited, Fakenham, Norfolk

Photography by John Lee
Line drawings by Rosemary Aldridge

ACKNOWLEDGEMENTS
The author and publishers thank the following
for their co-operation in supplying photographs for this book:
Allied Breweries Grants of St. James page 49
Birds Eye Foods Limited page 52
Pasta Foods Limited jacket and pages 17, 49, 53, 64
Pasta Information Centre pages 24–5, 29, 32, 56–7, 61
John West Foods Limited page 60
Dishes and accessories used in the photographs were kindly lent by
David Mellor, Ironmonger, 4 Sloane Square, London SW1 W8EE.

INTRODUCTION

Although it is a relatively new food in this country pasta has been around, according to museum records, since 5000 BC. It has been eaten in vast quantities for hundreds of years in Italy, although oddly enough while the consumption of pasta has increased in Western European countries and the United States it has fallen slightly in Italy recently. It is interesting to compare the pasta intake of various countries:

U.K. 1·5 lb. per head of population per annum

GERMANY 7·5 lb. per head of population per annum

U.S.A. 9·5 lb. per head of population per annum

FRANCE 15 lb. per head of population per annum

SWITZERLAND 21 lb. per head of population per annum

ITALY 66 lb. per head of population per annum

Some years ago I worked for a company who produced the raw materials from which pasta is made. One of my tasks was to help promote the use of pasta in the United Kingdom. At this time most people thought of pasta as school macaroni pudding and the spaghetti which you could buy in tins. It was enormously interesting and rewarding to demonstrate this food, which was so new and had so much variety to add to the menu, to audiences all over the country. Although I find the ever-increasing popularity of pasta very gratifying, I still do not feel that its potential for adding variety to our everyday menus has been fully realised.

The other great plus for pasta is that it is still cheap to buy and there is absolutely no waste. In these days of inflated prices I am very glad that my family are enthusiastic pasta eaters. Meals which can have rice, pasta or potatoes as accompaniments ring the changes, and a working housewife like myself is always pleased with the chance to avoid peeling the potatoes!

The continental cook recognises the necessity of meals which are budget-conscious as well as nutritious and serves pasta alongside meat, fish and poultry. Good pasta well cooked is a delight to eat and many of the different shapes are excellent with certain sauces and stews. The high protein content and the nutrients contained in it are higher than many other cooked vegetables. Contrary to many people's belief, pasta is no more fattening than many vegetables, and in fact it has fewer calories per ounce than some. Providing it is accompanied by salad and followed by fruit and cheese, it makes an excellent balanced meal for calorie counters!

The Italians have enough pasta shapes to eat a different one each day for over a year while we can call upon 40 shapes which are easily available and many more which are only available in specialised shops. Do buy good-quality pasta made from hard wheat as this gives a finished dish which has flavour, and is worth eating when it has been cooked with care.

I hope that this book will help you to extend your menus for family and friends, and enable you to develop your own pasta recipes when you have tried some of mine.

Myra Street

Acknowledgement

I would like to extend my grateful thanks to Jenny Roe, the consultant home economist to Pasta Foods Limited, St. Albans, for her help with the creating and testing of some of the recipes in the book.

I would also like to thank the Pasta Information Centre and Pasta Foods for their advice and co-operation and help with photographs.

NOTE ON METRICATION

In this book quantities have been given in both metric and Imperial measures. Exact conversion from Imperial to metric measures does not usually give very convenient working quantities and so for greater convenience we have rounded off metric measures into units of 25 grammes. The table below shows recommended equivalents.

Ounces/fluid ounces	Approx. g. and ml. to nearest whole figure	Recommended conversion to nearest unit of 25
1	28	25
2	57	50
3	85	75
4	113	100
5 ($\frac{1}{4}$ pint)	142	150
6	170	175
7	198	200
8 ($\frac{1}{2}$ lb.)	226	225
9	255	250
10 ($\frac{1}{2}$ pint)	283	275
11	311	300
12	340	350
13	368	375
14	396	400
15 ($\frac{3}{4}$ pint)	428	425
16 (1 lb.)	456	450
17	484	475
18	512	500
19	541	550
20 (1 pint)	569	575

Note When converting quantities over 20 oz. first add the appropriate figures in the centre column, *then* adjust to the nearest unit of 25. As a general guide, 1 kg. (1000 g.) equals 2·2 lb. or about 2 lb. 3 oz.; 1 litre (1000 ml.) equals 1·76 pints or almost exactly 1$\frac{3}{4}$ pints.

Liquid measures

The millilitre is a very small unit of measurement and we felt that to use decilitres (units of 100 ml.) would be less cumbersome. In most cases it is perfectly satisfactory to round off the exact millilitre conversion to the nearest decilitre, except for $\frac{1}{4}$ pint; thus $\frac{1}{4}$ pint (142 ml.) is 1$\frac{1}{2}$ dl., $\frac{1}{2}$ pint (283 ml.) is 3 dl., $\frac{3}{4}$ pint (428 ml.) is 4 dl., and 1 pint (569 ml.) is 6 dl. For quantities over 1 pint we have used litres and fractions of a litre.

Can sizes

Because at present cans are marked with the exact (usually to the nearest whole number) metric equivalent of the Imperial weight of the contents, we have followed this practice when giving can sizes. Thus the equivalent of a 14-oz. can of tomatoes would be a 396-g. can.

OVEN TEMPERATURES

The chart below gives recommended Celsius (Centigrade) equivalents.

Description	Fahrenheit	Celsius	Gas Mark
Very cool	225	110	$\frac{1}{4}$
	250	130	$\frac{1}{2}$
Cool	275	140	1
	300	150	2
Moderate	325	170	3
	350	180	4
Moderately hot	375	190	5
	400	200	6
Hot	425	220	7
	450	230	8
Very hot	475	240	9

NOTES FOR AMERICAN USERS

In the recipes in this book quantities are given in American standard cup and spoon measures as well as Imperial and metric measures. The list below gives some American equivalents or substitutes for terms or ingredients.

BRITISH	AMERICAN
basin	bowl
fillet	tenderloin
frying pan	skillet
greaseproof paper	wax paper
kitchen paper	paper towels
liquidiser	blender
mince	grind
minced beef	ground beef
pie dish	baking dish
pie plate	pie pan
stoned	pitted
whisk	beat/whip

NOTES FOR AUSTRALIAN USERS

Quantities in the recipes in this book are given in metric, Imperial and American measures. The old Australian standard measuring cup is the same as the American standard 8-fluid ounce cup; the new Australian cup is bigger and holds 250 ml. Note also that the Australian standard tablespoon holds 20 ml. and is therefore bigger than either the American (14·2 ml.) or the Imperial (17·7 ml.). The table below gives a comparison.

AMERICAN	BRITISH	AUSTRALIAN
1 teaspoon	1 teaspoon	1 teaspoon
1 tablespoon	1 tablespoon	1 tablespoon
3 tablespoons	2 tablespoons	2 tablespoons
4 tablespoons	3$\frac{1}{2}$ tablespoons	3 tablespoons
5 tablespoons	4 tablespoons	3$\frac{1}{2}$ tablespoons

THE STORY OF PASTA

Pasta is the generic term for the many products made from a dough of water and semolina which has been milled from the heart of the hardiest and purest of all wheats. It is kneaded into a paste, rolled out or extruded through a shape called a die and then cut and dried in a special way.

There are many interesting stories recorded about the origins of pasta, and a popular theory is that it was invented in China about 6000 years ago. It is said that pasta was first introduced to the Italians by Marco Polo when he returned from his travels in China in 1295. The climate of Italy was ideal for the producing of pasta and it fast became the staple diet of Italy.

The Italians feel almost as strongly about pasta as they do about opera and there is now a pasta museum near the Italian Riviera which was started by a family who made pasta into an industry in Italy around 1824. Here one can learn many fascinating things and examine the original as well as the modern machinery used in the manufacturing process.

The museum records show, despite the Marco Polo theory, that ravioli and noodles were being eaten in Rome in 1284, some years before Marco Polo returned to Italy. There are paintings and etchings showing the pasta being made in large sheets as well as gay dancing peasants eating long streamers of pasta in the streets. Ancient documents say that pasta was a revered and ancient food eaten as early as 5000 BC. Many poets and writers such as Rossini, Rabelais and Goldoni have sung the praises of pasta. The museum records a list of pasta names with English translations which are quite incredible. On pages 6 and 7 you will find drawings showing the most common modern shapes with their English and Italian names.

It is thought that Thomas Jefferson first introduced pasta into America in about 1786 when he returned from a tour of duty as American Ambassador to France. He is supposed to have brought back a spaghetti die from Italy and used it to make small amounts of spaghetti for his own personal use. However, it did not appear commercially in the States until about 1848 and only really established itself as an industry during the First World War when all imports from Italy were cut off.

The immigration in the nineteenth century of many people from Russia, Poland and Germany who brought with them a taste for noodles started an interest in pasta in this country. However, the actual manufacture of pasta in Britain only evolved gradually from about the beginning of this century when Italian shopkeepers began to sell fresh spaghetti, ravioli, noodles, etc., over the counter mainly around the Soho area of London.

The first full-scale manufacture of pasta made from durum semolina was started by H. J. Heinz Limited, who imported durum semolina. Then, in 1937, durum wheat for milling durum semolina, the raw material for pasta, was imported to Britain by a mill in Chelsea, London. This was the foundation of the manufacture of pasta made from durum semolina milled in this country. During the Second World War a number of other millers started to mill durum semolina, and since then the pasta industry has developed steadily until now some British pasta is exported to Europe and even the United States.

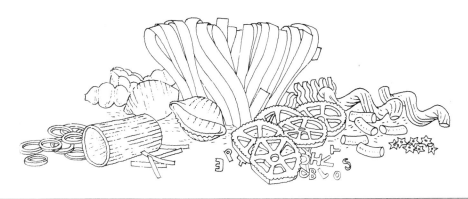

SHORT PASTA

small rings/anellini

medium rings

large rings

giant rings

tubetti

ditalini

ditali

penne and ziti tagliati

elbow macaroni/gramigna

elbow tubetti

corrugated macaroni/gramigna rigata

straight pipe macaroni (short cut)

large elbow macaroni/chifferoni

waggon wheels/ruote

squares

short cut buccatini

stars/stellette

small wheels

rigatoni

large rigatoni/grosso rigato

folded vermicelli

long vermicelli/fidelini

long spaghetti

folded fine noodles/fettuccini *folded broad noodles/tagliatelle* *lasagne*

SHORT PASTA
continued

lumache

miniature shells

cocks combs

soup noodles

spirals/tortiglioni

medium shells

grills

fideli

twistetti/eliche

shells/conchiglie

rice shapes/puntette

spaghettini (short cut spaghetti)

spiral macaroni

lumachine

melon seeds/semini di melo

alphabets

ЂOШ TO COOK PASTA

Pasta, like most other foods, will most certainly be ruined by bad cooking. As it is a very simple food to cook it does not always receive the careful attention which it deserves to make it into a really delicious meal. I have already talked about the importance of choosing good quality pasta made of hard wheat. Pasta made of softer wheats will make the cooking water cloudy and the resultant pasta will be soft and mushy without the distinctive nutty flavour of good pasta. Making your own pasta is great fun and worth the effort when you have mastered the kneading; however, for most of us leading busy lives, good-quality dried pasta is what we are going to cook most. I do hope that you will try the recipe for making your own later in the book.

You may have been puzzled by the cooking instructions for spaghetti in some Italian cookbooks. Most of these suggest that we use 7–8 quarts (8–9 litres) of boiling water for 1 lb. (450 g.) pasta. For those of you who have forgotten your tables that means at least 14 pints of water. Where on earth is anyone with a small modern kitchen going to keep a saucepan this size? The average large saucepan holds 6 pints (3½ litres), the larger size 8 pints (4½ litres). Very few people nowadays can run to anything larger. I have always managed to cook my pound of spaghetti in my large 8-pint saucepan. I am not saying that this is absolutely correct but it works!

Coil the spaghetti into a saucepan of rapidly boiling salted water.

Test a few strands after 10–12 minutes.

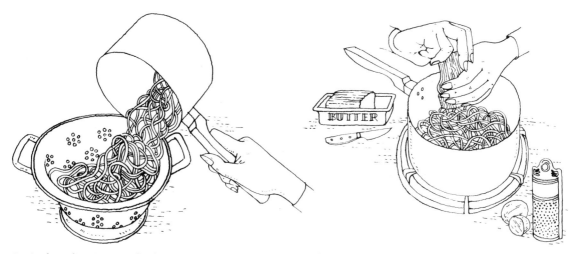

Drain through a sieve or colander.

Melt a knob of butter in the pan and return the spaghetti; sprinkle with pepper and nutmeg.

1 Bring a saucepan of water to the boil and when the water is bubbling throw in 1 tablespoon salt for 12 oz. (350 g.) pasta. Add 1 tablespoon oil to the water as this will prevent the pasta strands from sticking together.

2 Coil the pasta into the saucepan keeping the water on the boil all the time or throw the pasta shapes into the water if cooking smaller pasta.

3 Stir with a wooden fork to ensure that the strands do not stick together. Do this gently otherwise the pasta will be mashed.

4 Read directions on the packs for cooking times. Spaghetti will take 10–15 minutes, short cut shapes take about 8–12 minutes.

5 To test, take a little pasta out of the saucepan and bite. It should be firm or *al dente*, i.e., neither too hard with a white core through the centre nor too soft and mushy.

6 Drain through a sieve or colander. Melt a little butter in the saucepan and return the pasta. Shake with freshly ground pepper and a pinch of nutmeg.

There is another method of cooking pasta, by steaming it in a small amount of water. However, the traditional method is so simple that I cannot see much point in employing this steaming method, especially as I have known people to ruin saucepans by lack of timing.

TO SERVE PASTA WITH BUTTER AND CHEESE

The Italians often eat pasta as a starter or snack with butter and cheese or as an economy measure with oil and garlic. The latter is usually not palatable to British or American tastes, however for those who enjoy pasta as a starter it is worth trying if one has a taste for garlic. Pasta on its own with butter and cheese and even a little cream is delicious and has long been a favourite with my children who are not noted for their gourmet tastes!

For garlic lovers Cook 4 cloves garlic, finely chopped, in 1 tablespoon olive oil and $1\frac{1}{2}$ oz. (40 g., 3 tablespoons) butter slowly until soft but not brown. Mix with 2 tablespoons chopped parsley and allow to simmer for 1–2 minutes. Mix with 8 oz. (225 g.) cooked, drained spaghetti and serve piping hot with grated cheese.

For pasta lovers Add 2 oz. (50 g., $\frac{1}{2}$ cup) grated cheese, 2 oz. (50 g., $\frac{1}{4}$ cup) butter and 2 tablespoons cream to 8 oz. cooked, drained spaghetti or noodles (tagliatelle, for example), mix well and serve as a starter for 4–6 people.

Many people are daunted by the difficulty of eating spaghetti politely! These pictures show how it is done. Stick your fork into the spaghetti and twist it until a good mouthful is wound around the fork. Lift it up and pop it into your mouth; it is perfectly correct to bite off any trailing strands and let them drop back onto the plate.

SAUCES

When I think of sauces, the French immediately come to mind, and indeed they have contributed many of the famous sauces which we use every day in cookery. However it was the Italians who greatly influenced the development of French cookery in the sixteenth century, for at this time Venetian cooking was renowned. Even French historians have to admit that when Catherine de Medici came to the court of France to marry the Dauphin, Italian cooking was regarded as the best in Europe. This lady brought her cooks to the French court and history tells us that *haute cuisine* developed from this time.

The eating of pasta has developed through the ages in Italy and it is therefore to Italy that we must look for sauces which go well with pasta. The Italians criticise the French for the way they allow sauces to smother the food they are accompanying, and there is a valid lesson to be learnt from this for all of us who have just mastered a new and exciting sauce. Use fresh vegetables, subtle flavourings of herbs and garlic like the Italians do so that all the ingredients blend and the sauce is not dominated by one single ingredient.

It is easy to assume in this era of package holidays to the Adriatic and Mediterranean that all Italian sauces which accompany pasta are made of olive oil, garlic and tomato paste. This is far from the truth and I do hope that you will remember this if you are experimenting with different versions of these sauces. The creative cook can produce a different-tasting sauce each time by varying the ingredients and flavourings slightly. Sauces can be made in advance as they are easy to reheat and many are suitable for freezing. Boil-in-the-bag polythene is ideal for freezing and reheating sauces without dirtying saucepans.

GENOESE PESTO SAUCE

Preparation time 10–15 minutes or 2 minutes in a blender

AMERICAN	IMPERIAL/METRIC
1 oz. fresh basil leaves	1 oz./25 g. fresh basil leaves
2 cloves garlic	2 cloves garlic
generous pinch salt	generous pinch salt
½ cup pine kernels	2 oz./50 g. pine kernels
½ cup Parmesan cheese	2 oz./50 g. Parmesan cheese
about ½ cup olive oil	3–4 fl. oz./about 1 dl. olive oil
seasoning	seasoning

Pound the basil leaves in a mortar with the garlic, salt and pine kernels. Alternatively chop in a blender. Add the cheese. When the pesto is a thick purée begin to add the oil, a little at a time. When sufficient oil has been added the sauce should be of the same consistency as creamed butter. Season to taste. Serve with freshly cooked spaghetti, allowing each person to stir the desired amount of pesto into his serving.

Cooking time 1 hour
Serves 4

AMERICAN	IMPERIAL/METRIC
1 large onion	1 large onion
1 carrot	1 carrot
1–2 cloves garlic	1–2 cloves garlic
3 tablespoons olive oil	2 tablespoons olive oil
1 cup lean ground beef	8 oz./225 g. lean minced beef
¼ cup chicken livers (optional)	2 oz./50 g. chicken livers (optional)
1 7-oz. can peeled plum tomatoes	1 7-oz./198-g. can peeled plum tomatoes
¼ cup tomato paste	3 tablespoons tomato purée
⅔ cup water, bouillon or bouillon and red wine	¼ pint/1½ dl. water, stock or stock and red wine
salt and pepper	salt and pepper
½ teaspoon dried oregano	½ teaspoon dried oregano
1 bay leaf	1 bay leaf

Chop finely or grate the onion, carrot and garlic. Heat the oil in a saucepan and sauté the vegetables without browning for a few minutes. Add the garlic then add the minced beef and finely chopped chicken livers and allow to brown gently. Add all the other ingredients and allow to simmer for at least 45 minutes. Check the liquid carefully during cooking to make sure the sauce does not dry up. Serve with hot buttered pasta, with grated cheese handed separately.

MAYONNAISE

Makes ½ pint (3 dl., 1¼ cups)

AMERICAN	IMPERIAL/METRIC
1 whole egg	1 whole egg
salt and pepper	salt and pepper
¼ teaspoon French mustard	¼ teaspoon French mustard
3 tablespoons wine vinegar or lemon juice	2 tablespoons wine vinegar or lemon juice
1¼ cups vegetable oil, preferably olive	½ pint/3 dl. vegetable oil, preferably olive

For blender mayonnaise use the whole egg. Make sure all ingredients are at room temperature, i.e., do not use an egg which has just come out of the refrigerator. Put the egg in the goblet with the salt, pepper, mustard and 1 tablespoon vinegar, cover, and run on minimum speed. Pour in half of the oil very slowly while the machine is running. Stop the motor and add the remaining vinegar or lemon juice, then switch on to maximum speed and pour in the remainder of the oil.

Variation

Alternatively mayonnaise may be made with a hand mixer or a wooden spoon using the above ingredients but only the yolk of the egg. Place the egg yolk in a small bowl with the salt, pepper and mustard, mix and drop in the oil very slowly. Add vinegar or lemon juice at the end when a thick emulsion has been obtained.

MILANESE SAUCE

Cooking time 5 minutes
Makes generous ½ pint (3 dl., 1¼ cups)

AMERICAN	IMPERIAL/METRIC
1 cup mushrooms	4 oz./100 g. mushrooms
2 tablespoons butter	1 oz. butter
1¼ cups tomato sauce (see page 12)	½ pint/3 dl. tomato sauce (see page 12)
½ cup chopped cooked ham	4 oz./100 g. cooked ham, chopped

Sauté the mushrooms in the butter for several minutes then add the sauce. Lastly stir in the ham. Allow to simmer for a few minutes, then serve with 8 oz. (225 g.) cooked pasta which has been tossed in butter.

TOMATO SAUCE

Cooking time 30 minutes
Makes 1 pint

AMERICAN	IMPERIAL/METRIC
1 15-oz. can peeled plum tomatoes	1 15-oz./425-g. can peeled plum tomatoes
1 medium-sized onion	1 medium-sized onion
2 tablespoons butter	1 oz./25 g. butter
1 tablespoon oil	1 tablespoon oil
2 cloves garlic	2 cloves garlic
$\frac{1}{4}$ teaspoon mixed dried herbs or 1 bay leaf and a sprig marjoram and rosemary	$\frac{1}{4}$ teaspoon mixed dried herbs or 1 bay leaf and a sprig marjoram and rosemary
$\frac{2}{3}$ cup bouillon	$\frac{1}{4}$ pint/$1\frac{1}{2}$ dl. stock
salt and freshly ground black pepper	salt and freshly ground black pepper
1 tablespoon tomato paste	1 tablespoon tomato purée
knob butter	knob butter

Put the tomatoes and sliced onion in a saucepan with the butter and oil, then add the chopped cloves of garlic, the herbs and stock. Season well, cover and simmer until the sauce is thick and pulpy. Put through a blender, food mill or sieve. Add the tomato purée, stir in the knob of butter and boil until thick.

Variation
FRESH TOMATO SAUCE

Instead of using canned tomatoes you can use 2 lb. (900 g.) fresh tomatoes. Peel them by dipping quickly in boiling water then removing the skins, and cut into eight pieces. Simmer gently with the other ingredients until the tomatoes are soft. Alternatively the tomatoes may be blended or sieved first, then simmered.

Tomato sauce can be frozen in plastic boxes or polythene bags, but I usually add a fresh sprig of herbs on reheating.

CELERY AND HAM SAUCE

Cooking time 20 minutes
Serves 4

AMERICAN	IMPERIAL/METRIC
$\frac{1}{3}$ lb. unsmoked ham, butt half	6 oz./175 g. green gammon
3 stalks celery	3 stalks celery
1 carrot	1 carrot
1 small clove garlic	1 small clove garlic
3 tablespoons butter	$1\frac{1}{2}$ oz./40 g. butter
1 tablespoon flour	1 tablespoon flour
3 tablespoons tomato paste	2 tablespoons tomato purée
$1\frac{1}{4}$ cups chicken bouillon	$\frac{1}{2}$ pint/3 dl. chicken stock
black pepper	black pepper
1 tablespoon Parmesan cheese	1 tablespoon Parmesan cheese

Chop the gammon, celery and carrot, crush the clove of garlic. Melt the butter and sauté the bacon gently for 3–4 minutes. Add the vegetables and garlic, cover and sauté for a further 3–4 minutes. Stir in the flour. Cook well then gradually add the tomato purée and stock. Season with pepper and cook for 10 minutes. Serve sprinkled with Parmesan cheese.

BECHAMEL SAUCE

Cooking time 8 minutes
Makes 1 pint (6 dl., 2½ cups)

AMERICAN	IMPERIAL/METRIC
2½ cups milk	1 pint/6 dl. milk
1 bay leaf	1 bay leaf
3 tablespoons butter	1½ oz./45 g. butter
6 tablespoons flour	1½ oz./45 g. flour
salt and pepper	salt and pepper

Heat the milk slowly in a saucepan with the bay leaf. Meanwhile melt the butter in another saucepan until it begins to sizzle, but do not allow it to brown. Add the flour and stir into the butter quickly; keep stirring until a roux (see note) is formed. Remove the bay leaf from the milk and stir some into the roux, then heat, stirring all the time, until the sauce is smooth and thickened. Use a wooden spoon only, or if you are afraid of lumps a small, spoon-shaped wire whisk is ideal. Gradually add the remaining milk until a smooth creamy sauce is obtained. Season and simmer for several minutes to cook the sauce thoroughly. Before using taste for seasoning.

Note A roux is a paste made by combining the flour with the melted fat over heat so that the flour cooks.

MUSHROOM AND LEMON SAUCE

Cooking time about 20 minutes
Serves 6–8

AMERICAN	IMPERIAL/METRIC
2½ cups milk	1 pint/6 dl. milk
1 carrot	1 carrot
1 onion studded with 2 cloves	1 onion studded with 2 cloves
1 stalk celery	1 stalk celery
1½ cups mushrooms	6 oz./175 g. mushrooms
¼ cup butter	2 oz./50 g. butter
¾ cup flour	3 oz./75 g. flour
1¼ cups bouillon	½ pint/3 dl. chicken stock
3 tablespoons lemon juice	2 tablespoons lemon juice
1 can anchovy fillets	1 can anchovy fillets
generous ¼ cup grated cheese	1½ oz./40 g cheese, grated
salt and pepper	salt and pepper

Put the milk, carrot, onion and celery in a saucepan and bring to boiling point. Remove from the heat and leave to infuse for 15 minutes, then strain. Slice the mushrooms, melt the butter in a frying pan and sauté the mushrooms for 3–4 minutes, before adding the flour. Cook for 2 minutes before stirring in the stock, lemon juice and infused milk. Bring to the boil and simmer for 3–4 minutes. Drain and chop the anchovies and stir into the sauce together with the grated cheese. Season well and gently reheat.

To serve, cook some pasta as previously directed, drain and toss in butter and turn into a serving dish. Pour the mushroom sauce over the pasta or serve separately.

CURRY SAUCE

Cooking time 20 minutes
Makes ¼ pint (1½ dl., ⅔ cup)

AMERICAN	IMPERIAL/METRIC
½ small onion	½ small onion
2 teaspoons oil	2 teaspoons oil
2 teaspoons curry powder	2 teaspoons curry powder
⅔ cup bouillon	¼ pint/1½ dl. stock
1 teaspoon lemon juice	1 teaspoon lemon juice
1 teaspoon onion chutney	1 teaspoon onion chutney

Chop the onion finely and sauté in the oil until tender. Add the curry powder and cook for a further 2 minutes. Add the remaining ingredients and simmer, covered, for a further 10 minutes, then cool. Use this sauce with chopped cooked or minced meat, served with noodles or small shapes.

SOUPS

I am constantly amazed at the number of people who say that they never bother to make soup. Napoleon is supposed to have said, 'Soup makes soldiers', and on a dreary, wet, cold day I can certainly see what he meant. Try giving the family a steaming plate of broth and they will cheer up immediately. I have always been an avid believer in the stock pot but if you can't face the smell of boiling meat and bones then use bouillon cubes to give the vegetables flavour.

In the winter we nearly always have soup for a starter and now that I have a freezer I make large quantities, when I have time, and freeze at least two batches of each type. I find the children prefer lentil and vegetable broths to cream soups so I often make half broth and half cream from the same batch by sieving or liquidising for the cream variety. A little pasta added to soup makes it just that bit more nutritious and interesting and turns soup into an ideal light meal on its own. Do not add pasta to soup if you are going to freeze it, but add it on reheating.

Soup is very little trouble to prepare; many people have gadgets for chopping vegetables which make the preparation very easy. Although tinned and packaged soups are very convenient they are expensive if you have a family of three or more. Babies can be introduced to home-made soup if you season lightly then remove the baby's portion and season the remainder again before serving.

The Italians are more adventurous than we are with soup and use many different fresh vegetables. Soups are often thickened with pasta or rice. The idea of serving *crostini* (rounds of bread spread with cheese and heated in the oven until golden and crisp) seems to have originated in Italy and really makes soup into a meal.

ITALIAN VEGETABLE BROTH

Cooking time 50 minutes
Serves 4–6

AMERICAN	IMPERIAL/METRIC
1 onion	1 onion
2 small carrots	2 small carrots
1 small turnip	1 small turnip
1 small green sweet pepper	1 small green pepper
1 leek	1 leek
2 bouillon cubes	2 stock cubes
6 cups water	2½ pints/1¼ litres water
seasoning	seasoning
½ cup pasta alphabets	2 oz./50 g. pasta alphabets
3 tablespoons chopped parsley	2 tablespoons chopped parsley

Wash the vegetables and chop into small pieces, keeping the leek separate. Make up the stock with the stock cubes and water (or use stock for this if you have some), then add the onion, carrots, turnip (do not use too much turnip; if small new turnips are not available use only a small piece) and green pepper. Bring to the boil and simmer for 20 minutes. Add the leek and simmer for a further 10 minutes; season to taste. Add the pasta to the boiling soup and simmer until tender. Sprinkle generously with parsley and serve with fresh crusty bread. This soup may also be served with grated cheese.

MINESTRONE

Cooking time 45 minutes
Serves 6–8

AMERICAN	IMPERIAL/METRIC
¼ cup navy beans	2 oz./50 g. dried haricot beans
¼ cup dried lentils	2 oz./50 g. dried lentils
3 tablespoons oil	2 tablespoons oil
1 cup diced salt pork	6 oz./175 g. salt pork, diced
1 large onion	1 large onion
1 lb. 13-oz. can plum tomatoes	1 lb. 13-oz./822-g. can plum tomatoes
2½ quarts bouillon	4 pints/2¼ litres stock
2 carrots	2 carrots
1 medium-sized potato	1 medium-sized potato
2 leeks	2 leeks
1 teaspoon salt	1 teaspoon salt
¼ teaspoon pepper	¼ teaspoon pepper
½ small firm white cabbage	½ small firm white cabbage
½ cup frozen peas	2 oz./50 g. frozen peas
½ cup ditali	2 oz./50 g. ditali
grated Parmesan or any hard cheese	grated Parmesan or any hard cheese

Soak the beans and lentils for several hours in cold water. Heat the oil in a large saucepan and add the diced salt pork; fry until fairly crisp. Add the finely chopped onion and sauté until soft. Add the tomatoes and stir the mixture with a wooden spoon to break down the tomatoes. Add the stock, drained lentils and beans. Cut the carrots and potato into small dice; cut the leeks into small slices, add to the soup and season. Bring to the boil and simmer for 25 minutes. Shred the cabbage and add with the peas. Cook for 5 minutes then add the pasta. Serve when the pasta is cooked, with grated cheese sprinkled on top and accompanied by freshly heated crispy bread.

This soup freezes well and it is a meal in itself. However, if you are making enough to freeze, freeze without pasta and add on reheating.

FISH SOUP

Cooking time 1 hour 40 minutes
Serves 6

AMERICAN	IMPERIAL/METRIC
1 onion	1 onion
1 carrot	1 carrot
1 leek	1 leek
1 bulb Florentine fennel if available	1 head Florence fennel if available
generous quart mussels	2 pints/generous litre mussels
⅔ cup dry white wine	¼ pint/1½ dl. dry white wine
2 tablespoons melted butter	1 oz./25 g. melted butter
1–2 cloves garlic	1–2 cloves garlic
½ lb. cod or other white fish	8 oz./225 g. cod or rock salmon
2 oz. vermicelli	2 oz./50 g. vermicelli
salt and pepper	salt and pepper
¼ cup chopped parsley	3 tablespoons chopped parsley
Fish stock	
fish trimmings – heads, tails, etc.	fish trimmings – heads, tails, etc.
1 onion	1 onion
2 bay leaves	2 bay leaves
2 quarts water	3 pints/1¾ litres water
1 teaspoon dried fennel	1 teaspoon dried fennel
bacon rinds if available	bacon rinds if available

First make the stock. Put the fish trimmings, onion and bay leaves into the water with the dried herbs and bacon rinds. Bring to the boil and simmer for nearly 1 hour. Meanwhile prepare the vegetables by peeling them first. Chop the onion, dice the carrot and slice the leek. Cut the fennel into small strips. Wash the mussels, remove the beards and put in a saucepan with a little of the white wine over a low heat until the mussels open. Place the chopped onion in a large soup saucepan with the melted butter. Add the carrot, fennel and chopped or crushed garlic. Strain over the fish stock and cook for 15 minutes, then add the leek and white fish and cook for another 15 minutes. Add the remaining wine and the mussels, cook for a further few minutes then add the vermicelli. Season to taste, simmer for 4–5 minutes, then serve with hot garlic bread. Sprinkle each portion of soup with chopped parsley.

LENTIL SOUP

Cooking time 2 hours
Serves 6–8

AMERICAN	IMPERIAL/METRIC
1 cup dried lentils	8 oz./225 g. dried lentils
3 quarts chicken bouillon	5 pints/2¾ litres chicken stock
4 slices bacon	4 rashers bacon
1 teaspoon salt	1 teaspoon salt
freshly milled black pepper	freshly milled black pepper
4 onions	4 onions
6 stalks celery	6 stalks celery
⅓ cup oil	4 tablespoons oil
½ cup small pasta	2 oz./50 g. small pasta

Soak the lentils in cold water for a few hours, drain well. Bring the stock to the boil in a large saucepan, add the lentils and the bacon cut in pieces, season well. Allow to simmer for about 1½ hours. Chop the onions finely and the celery into thin pieces. Heat the oil in a frying pan and gently fry the onions and celery until golden brown but do not allow any of the pieces to burn. Add the onions and celery to the soup and simmer for a further 15 minutes. Add the pasta, check the seasoning and serve when the pasta is cooked.

CHICKEN-NOODLE SOUP

Cooking time 40 minutes
Serves 4–6

AMERICAN	IMPERIAL/METRIC
2 quarts chicken bouillon	3 pints/1¾ litres chicken stock
2 carrots	2 carrots
2 stalks celery, chopped	2 stalks celery, chopped
3 scallions	3 spring onions
seasoning	seasoning
1 cup sliced mushrooms	4 oz./100 g. mushrooms
½ cup small pasta shells or noodles	2 oz./50 g. small pasta shells or noodles
½ cup cooked diced chicken	4 oz./100 g. cooked chicken, diced

Bring the stock to boiling point and toss in the diced carrots, chopped celery and spring onions. Add a little salt and pepper and simmer for 15 minutes. Add the sliced mushrooms and pasta and stir carefully with a wooden spoon. Add the chicken and simmer for a further 15 minutes.

QUICK SPINACH SOUP

Cooking time 30 minutes
Serves 4–6

AMERICAN	IMPERIAL/METRIC
5 cups beef bouillon	2 pints/generous litre beef broth
½ cup pasta rings	2 oz./50 g. pasta rings
1 cup chopped cooked spinach (see note)	8 oz./225 g. chopped cooked spinach (see note)
seasoning	seasoning
2 egg yolks, beaten	2 egg yolks, beaten
3 tablespoons grated Parmesan cheese	2 tablespoons grated Parmesan cheese
bread and cheese, toasted	bread and cheese, toasted

Make up the beef broth using 2 beef stock cubes. Bring to the boil and add the pasta rings, simmer gently for about 7 minutes. Add the spinach and seasoning and simmer for a further 10 minutes. Bring to the boil and remove from the heat. Add a little of the boiling broth to the egg yolks and then blend the egg mixture into the soup. Serve in bowls with toasted bread and cheese floating on top, or with crisp crusty bread.

Note The spinach may be frozen, fresh or left over from a previous meal.

Tagliatelle

STARTERS & QUICK MEALS

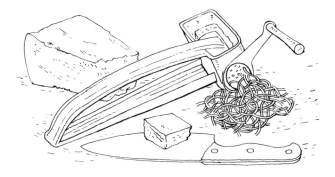

Pasta is a marvellous starter for those who have hearty appetites. I find that a very small amount is an excellent starter and most people find it beyond them to eat very much if they are going on to a main course. Pasta can be served on its own with butter and cheese or with a sauce. Parmesan cheese is excellent to serve with pasta or a mixture of Gruyère and Parmesan is also very tasty, but any fairly strong hard cheese will do. Lasagne or cannelloni is often served as a starter but I must say I prefer to enjoy it as a main course as even a small portion is fairly filling.

Pasta dishes are ideal for quick meals, suppers or high teas and as many of the dishes in this chapter are suitable for either starters or suppers I have put them all together. A quick sauce can be made while you cook your pasta.

CANNELLONI

Cooking time   30–35 minutes
Oven temperature   350°F., 180°C., Gas Mark 4
Serves   6

AMERICAN	IMPERIAL/METRIC
12 tubes cannelloni	12 tubes cannelloni
seasoning	seasoning
1 tablespoon oil	1 tablespoon oil
1 lb. frozen chopped spinach	1 lb./450 g. frozen chopped spinach
1 tablespoon cream (optional)	1 tablespoon cream (optional)
1 cup cottage cheese	8 oz./225 g. cottage cheese
3 slices cooked ham, diced	3 slices cooked ham, diced

Cheese sauce

6 tablespoons butter	3 oz./75 g. butter
¾ cup flour	3 oz./75 g. flour
3¾ cups milk	1½ pints/scant litre milk
salt and pepper	salt and pepper
pinch grated nutmeg	pinch grated nutmeg
1½ cups grated Emmenthal cheese	6 oz./175 g. Emmenthal cheese, grated
3 tablespoons bread crumbs	2 tablespoons breadcrumbs
1 tablespoon grated Parmesan cheese	1 tablespoon grated Parmesan cheese

Illustrated on page 52

Cook the cannelloni in boiling salted water which has had at least 1 tablespoon oil added to prevent the tubes from sticking together. Drain and dry on kitchen paper. The cannelloni will probably need to be cooked in batches unless you have a very large saucepan. Cook the frozen spinach as directed, drain well, add seasoning and, if you feel extravagant, 1 tablespoon cream. Mix the spinach with the cottage cheese and ham and spoon into the cannelloni. Arrange in an ovenproof dish.

To make the sauce, melt the butter in a saucepan and stir in the flour to make a roux. Add the milk and stir until a smooth sauce is formed, season to taste. Add the nutmeg and Emmenthal cheese and pour the sauce over the pasta. Put into a moderate oven to heat for 15 minutes, then remove and sprinkle with a mixture of breadcrumbs and Parmesan. Brown the whole dish under the grill. This makes an excellent supper dish with a crisp salad.

Freeze this dish in a shallow container with a lid or cover with foil so that it can go from the freezer to the oven.

GREEN NOODLE DOUGH

Cooking time 3–4 minutes
Makes 1 lb. (450 g.) noodles

AMERICAN	IMPERIAL/METRIC
4 cups all-purpose flour	1 lb./450 g. plain flour
1 teaspoon salt	1 teaspoon salt
4 eggs	4 eggs
1 tablespoon olive oil or vegetable oil	1 tablespoon olive oil or vegetable oil
1 cup cooked shredded spinach	8 oz./225 g. cooked shredded spinach

Work as for ravioli paste until a firm dough is obtained, including the spinach which should be squeezed dry. Then knead by hand or with the dough hook on the mixer until smooth and elastic. Divide into three pieces and roll out thinly as shown on page 22. Cut into strips, cover with a clean cloth and leave for 1–2 hours. Cook in boiling salted water for about 4 minutes. This dough will also make lasagne. Cut out 3-inch (7½-cm.) squares. Allow to dry on a cloth for 1–2 hours; cook for about 3 minutes in boiling salted water. Use in any lasagne recipe, e.g., lasagne verdi.

LASAGNE VERDI

Cooking time 30–40 minutes
Oven temperature 350°F., 180°C., Gas Mark 4
Serves 6

AMERICAN	IMPERIAL/METRIC
12 sheets lasagne verdi	12 sheets lasagne verdi
1 tablespoon oil	1 tablespoon oil
bolognese sauce (see page 11)	bolognese sauce (see page 11)
4 cups béchamel sauce (see page 13)	1½ pints/scant litre béchamel sauce (see page 13)
¼–½ cup grated cheese	1–2 oz./25–50 g. cheese, grated

Cook the lasagne in boiling salted water with the oil. Bought dried lasagne will take longer to cook than fresh, therefore follow cooking directions on the packet. Drain the lasagne on sheets of clean kitchen paper, then use to line a greased 10-inch (25-cm.) round earthenware dish, about 1½ inches (4 cm.) in depth, or a square or oblong casserole or pyrex dish; do not overlap. Spread with a layer of bolognese sauce and a layer of béchamel sauce. Continue the layers of lasagne, bolognese sauce and béchamel sauce until the ingredients are used up. The number of layers will depend on the size of the dish, however, do not use more than three. Finish with a layer of the two sauces and sprinkle with grated cheese. Bake in a moderate oven until golden brown and bubbling, about 20–30 minutes.

Illustrated on page 20 and the jacket

TAGLIATELLE WITH EGG-CREAM SAUCE

Cooking time 15 minutes
Serves 6–8

AMERICAN	IMPERIAL/METRIC
1½ lb. tagliatelle	1½ lb./675 g. tagliatelle
8 egg yolks	8 egg yolks
½ cup heavy cream	scant ¼ pint/1 dl. double cream
½ cup butter, cut into very small pieces	4 oz./100 g. butter, cut into very small pieces
1 teaspoon salt	1 teaspoon salt
1½ teaspoons pepper	1½ teaspoons pepper
½ cup grated Parmesan cheese	2 oz./50 g. Parmesan cheese, grated

Cook the tagliatelle in boiling salted water and drain well. Beat the egg yolks in a saucepan. Add the cream, butter, salt, pepper and cheese. Mix well. Add the pasta, tossing lightly over a very low heat until the butter melts and the tagliatelle is well coated.

Lasagne verdi (see page 19) and spaghetti bolognese (see page 76)

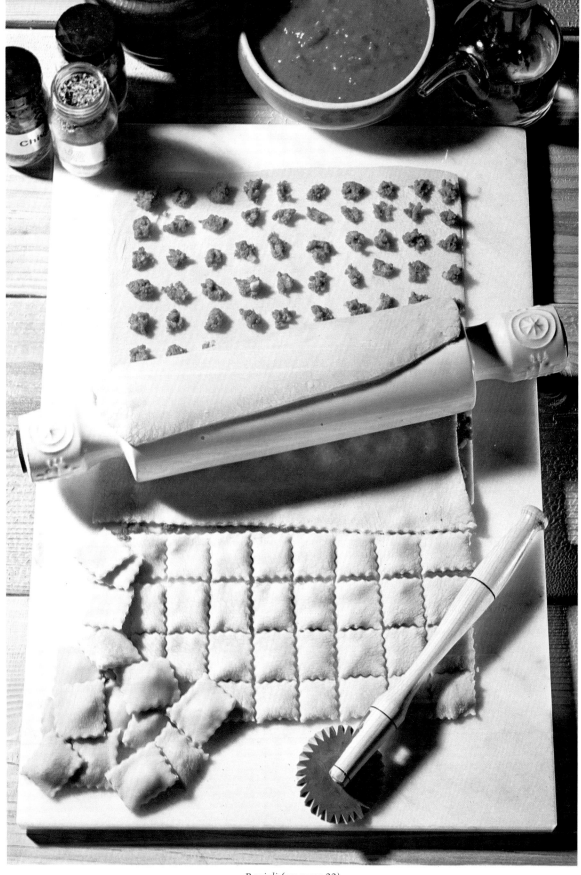

Ravioli (see page 22)

Cooking time about 10 minutes according to size
Serves 4–6

AMERICAN	IMPERIAL/METRIC
2 cups all-purpose flour	8 oz./225 g. plain flour
good $\frac{1}{4}$ teaspoon salt	good $\frac{1}{4}$ teaspoon salt
1 egg	1 egg
1 tablespoon olive oil	1 tablespoon olive oil
$\frac{1}{4}$ cup warm water	3 tablespoons warm water
bolognese sauce (see page 11)	bolognese sauce (see page 11)
tomato sauce (see page 12)	tomato sauce (see page 12)

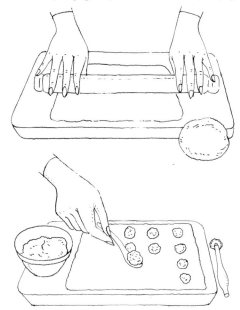

Illustrated on page 21

1 Sieve the flour onto a clean dry board or work top.

2 Make a well in the centre of the flour and put in the egg, oil and 2 tablespoons of the water.

3 Mix the dough gradually and pull in the flour from the sides of the well (same method as for shortbread). Add the remaining liquid as you need it to mix in more flour. Continue to work the paste until it is firm and smooth, kneading well for several minutes.

4 Cover with a cloth and leave to rest for $\frac{1}{2}$ hour.

5 Cut the paste in half and roll out one piece until it is as thin as you can make it without breaking the dough. Set aside and roll the other half of the paste to the same size.

6 Brush over one sheet with cold water and place drained bolognese sauce in little heaps with a teaspoon on the sheet of paste. Cover with the second sheet and press down round each mound of filling (see photograph on page 21).

7 Cut with a pastry wheel or a small fluted cutter. Put on a tray and allow to dry for about 2 hours before cooking. This is the ideal stage to freeze ravioli.

8 To cook, bring a large saucepan of water to boiling point, add salt and drop in the ravioli for 10–15 minutes. Serve accompanied by tomato sauce and grated cheese.

Variation

Ravioli may be filled with any kind of minced meat or chicken, mixed with onion, seasoned and flavoured with herbs. Alternatively, cream cheese and spinach make a delicious filling. Use 12 oz. (350 g.) fresh spinach or a small packet of frozen mixed with seasoning and 2 oz. (50 g., $\frac{1}{4}$ cup) cream cheese.

UMBRIAN SPAGHETTI

Cooking time 30 minutes
Serves 4–6

AMERICAN	IMPERIAL/METRIC
6 anchovies	6 anchovies
$\frac{1}{2}$ cup olive oil	6 tablespoons olive oil
2 cloves garlic, sliced	2 cloves garlic, sliced
1 tablespoon tomato paste	1 tablespoon tomato purée
$\frac{1}{2}$ cup water	scant $\frac{1}{4}$ pint/1 dl. water
$\frac{1}{2}$ teaspoon freshly ground black pepper	$\frac{1}{2}$ teaspoon freshly ground black pepper
1 lb. spaghetti	1 lb./450 g. spaghetti

Cover the anchovies with water and allow to soak for 10 minutes. Drain well and mash very finely. Heat the olive oil in a frying pan and sauté the garlic until brown. Discard the garlic. Add the anchovies, tomato purée, water and black pepper to the oil. Mix well together. Cook over a low heat for 30 minutes. Cook the spaghetti as directed and drain well. Check the seasoning, pour the sauce over the spaghetti, toss lightly and serve.

Cooking time 1 hour 20 minutes
Oven temperature 400°F., 200°C., Gas Mark 6
Serves 4–6

AMERICAN	IMPERIAL/METRIC
¼ lb. hot Italian sausage	4 oz./100 g. hot Italian sausage
¼ lb. sweet Italian sausage	4 oz./100 g. sweet Italian sausage
6 tablespoons olive oil	5 tablespoons olive oil
2 cloves garlic, finely chopped	2 cloves garlic, finely chopped
1 lb. 4-oz. can plum tomatoes, chopped	1 lb. 4-oz./567-g. can plum tomatoes, chopped
1 6-oz. can tomato paste	1 6-oz./175-g. can tomato purée
½ teaspoon basil	½ teaspoon basil
½ teaspoon salt	½ teaspoon salt
¼ teaspoon black pepper	¼ teaspoon black pepper
1 lb. lasagne	1 lb./450 g. lasagne
4 cups sliced mushrooms	1 lb./450 g. mushrooms, sliced
1 lb. ricotta cheese	1 lb./450 g. ricotta cheese
¾ lb. mozzarella cheese, sliced	12 oz./350 g. mozzarella cheese, sliced
¼ cup grated Parmesan cheese	1 oz. Parmesan cheese, grated

Remove the skin of the sausage and chop the meat. Lightly brown the sausage meat in a saucepan. Pour off the fat and add 3 tablespoons of the oil to the saucepan. Stir in the garlic for 1 minute, then add the tomatoes, tomato purée, basil, salt and pepper. Bring to the boil and cook over a low heat for 45 minutes, stirring frequently. Cook the lasagne in boiling salted water, adding 1 tablespoon oil to prevent sticking. Drain well and dry on kitchen paper. Sauté the mushrooms in the remaining oil for 5 minutes. In a shallow oiled baking dish, spread a layer of lasagne, then layers of ricotta, mozzarella, mushrooms and the sauce. Continue until all the ingredients are used, ending with the sauce. Sprinkle with the Parmesan cheese. Bake in a moderately hot oven for 20 minutes, or until very hot.

Cooking time 50 minutes
Serves 4–6

AMERICAN	IMPERIAL/METRIC
3 tablespoons olive oil	2 tablespoons olive oil
1 large onion, chopped	1 large onion, chopped
8 anchovy fillets, finely chopped	8 anchovy fillets, finely chopped
3 tablespoons chopped parsley	2 tablespoons chopped parsley
1 clove garlic, finely chopped	1 clove garlic, finely chopped
1 stalk celery, finely chopped	1 stalk celery, finely chopped
½ teaspoon rosemary	½ teaspoon rosemary
½ teaspoon sage	½ teaspoon sage
1 lb. tomatoes, skinned and diced	1 lb./450 g. tomatoes, skinned and diced
1 lb. spaghetti	1 lb./450 g. spaghetti
½ cup dry white wine	scant ¼ pint/1 dl. dry white wine
¾ teaspoon salt	¾ teaspoon salt
½ teaspoon black pepper	½ teaspoon black pepper
grated Parmesan or Romano cheese	grated Parmesan or Romano cheese

Heat the oil in a saucepan; sauté the onions for 10 minutes. Add the anchovies, parsley, garlic, celery, rosemary and sage and cook over a low heat for 5 minutes. Add the tomatoes and cook for 30 minutes. Cook the spaghetti and drain well. Mix the wine, salt and pepper into the sauce and cook for another minute. Taste for seasoning. Pour the sauce over the spaghetti and serve with the grated cheese.

Baked fish with pasta shells (see page 43)

SPAGHETTI CARBONARA

Cooking time about 15 minutes
Serves 4

AMERICAN	IMPERIAL/METRIC
$\frac{1}{2}$ lb. spaghetti	8 oz./225 g. spaghetti
1 onion	1 onion
$\frac{1}{2}$ cup mushrooms	2 oz./50 g. mushrooms
5 slices bacon	4 oz./100 g. bacon
$\frac{1}{4}$ cup butter	2 oz./50 g. butter
2 eggs	2 eggs
black pepper	black pepper
$\frac{1}{4}$ cup grated Parmesan cheese	1 oz./25 g. Parmesan cheese, grated
1 teaspoon chopped parsley	1 teaspoon chopped parsley

Cook the spaghetti in plenty of boiling, salted water for 10–12 minutes until tender. Finely slice the onion and mushrooms and dice the bacon. Drain the spaghetti, add 1 oz. (25 g., 2 tablespoons) of the butter and keep warm. Melt the remaining butter and sauté the onion, mushrooms and bacon. Whisk the eggs and add the black pepper and cheese. Mix the spaghetti with the bacon and vegetables and then add the egg mixture. Cook for a few moments until thick and creamy. Turn into a heated bowl and sprinkle with the parsley.

SPAGHETTI HOME STYLE

Cooking time 1 hour
Serves 4–6

AMERICAN	IMPERIAL/METRIC
$\frac{1}{4}$ lb. bacon	4 oz./100 g. bacon
1 onion, chopped	1 onion, chopped
1 clove garlic, finely chopped	1 clove garlic, finely chopped
1 stalk celery, chopped	1 stalk celery, chopped
1 carrot, grated	1 carrot, grated
$\frac{1}{4}$ cup tomato paste	3 tablespoons tomato purée
$1\frac{1}{2}$ cups water	generous $\frac{1}{2}$ pint/3 dl. water
$\frac{1}{4}$ teaspoon freshly ground black pepper	$\frac{1}{4}$ teaspoon freshly ground black pepper
$\frac{1}{2}$ tablespoon sugar	$\frac{1}{2}$ tablespoon sugar
1 lb. spaghetti	1 lb./450 g. spaghetti
2 tablespoons chopped parsley	2 tablespoons chopped parsley
2 tablespoons butter	1 oz. butter

Fry the chopped bacon in a saucepan for 2 minutes. Mix the onion, garlic, celery and carrot. Cook over a low heat for 10 minutes, stirring frequently. Mix in the tomato purée, water, pepper and sugar. Cook over a low heat for 45 minutes, stirring occasionally. Meanwhile, cook the spaghetti and drain well. Stir in the parsley and melted butter. Taste the sauce for seasoning. Heap the spaghetti onto a hot serving dish, pour the sauce over it and toss lightly. Serve immediately.

NOODLES WITH WALNUT SAUCE

Cooking time 15 minutes
Serves 4–6

AMERICAN	IMPERIAL/METRIC
1 lb. tagliatelle	1 lb./450 g. tagliatelle
1 clove garlic, finely chopped	1 clove garlic, finely chopped
1 cup ground walnuts	4 oz./100 g. ground walnuts
1 lb. ricotta cheese	1 lb./450 g. ricotta cheese
1 cup grated Parmesan cheese	4 oz./100 g. Parmesan cheese, grated
2 teaspoons salt	2 teaspoons salt
$\frac{1}{2}$ teaspoon pepper	$\frac{1}{2}$ teaspoon pepper

Cook the noodles in plenty of boiling salted water and drain well. Meanwhile, pound or roll the garlic and walnuts together until a paste is formed; alternatively place in a blender. Put in a bowl with the ricotta and Parmesan cheeses, salt and pepper. Add the hot noodles. Toss lightly with two forks until the noodles are coated with the nut mixture.

NOODLES ROMANOFF

Cooking time 45–50 minutes
Oven temperature 350°F., 180°C., Gas Mark 4
Serves 6

AMERICAN	IMPERIAL/METRIC
$\frac{1}{2}$ lb. egg noodles	8 oz./225 g. egg noodles
1 medium-sized onion	1 medium-sized onion
2 tablespoons butter	1 oz./25 g. butter
1 clove garlic	1 clove garlic
$\frac{1}{2}$ cup cottage cheese with chives	4 oz./100 g. cottage cheese with chives
$\frac{2}{3}$ cup cultured sour cream	$\frac{1}{4}$ pint/1$\frac{1}{2}$ dl. soured cream
2 teaspoons Worcestershire sauce	2 teaspoons Worcestershire sauce
dash Tabasco	dash Tabasco
salt and pepper	salt and pepper
1 cup grated Cheddar cheese	4 oz./100 g. Cheddar cheese, grated

Cook the noodles as previously directed. Dice the onion and sauté in the butter until tender but not coloured. Crush the garlic. Drain the noodles, mix them lightly with the sautéed onion, the garlic, cottage cheese, soured cream and seasonings. Turn into a greased baking dish. Grate the cheese and sprinkle over the noodles. Bake in a moderate oven for 30–40 minutes, until golden.

MACARONI LIVORNESE STYLE

Cooking time 1 hour
Oven temperature 375°F., 190°C., Gas Mark 5
Serves 4–6

AMERICAN	IMPERIAL/METRIC
$\frac{1}{4}$ cup butter	2 oz./50 g. butter
1$\frac{1}{2}$ lb. tomatoes, chopped	1$\frac{1}{2}$ lb./675 g. tomatoes, chopped
1 lb. macaroni	1 lb./450 g. macaroni
2 teaspoons salt	2 teaspoons salt
$\frac{1}{2}$ teaspoon pepper	$\frac{1}{2}$ teaspoon pepper
4 cups mushrooms	1 lb./450 g. mushrooms
2 tablespoons flour	$\frac{1}{2}$ oz./15 g. flour
scant 2 cups milk	$\frac{3}{4}$ pint/4 dl. milk
$\frac{1}{2}$ cup grated Parmesan cheese	2 oz./50 g. Parmesan cheese, grated
$\frac{1}{4}$ lb. mozzarella cheese, sliced	4 oz./100 g. mozzarella cheese, sliced

Melt half the butter in a skillet. Add the tomatoes. Cook over a low heat for 15 minutes, stirring frequently. Cook and drain the macaroni. Season the tomatoes with 1 teaspoon salt and $\frac{1}{4}$ teaspoon pepper. Melt the remaining butter in a saucepan. Sauté the mushrooms for 2 minutes, then sprinkle with the flour, stirring until smooth. Add the milk, stirring constantly until the sauce boils. Simmer over a low heat for 5 minutes. Add the remaining salt and pepper. Spread half the macaroni in a buttered baking dish. Cover with the tomatoes and then the mushroom mixture. Add the remaining macaroni. Sprinkle the Parmesan cheese over and arrange slices of mozzarella cheese on top. Bake in a moderate oven for 30 minutes.

MACARONI CHEESE FRITTERS

Cooking time 10 minutes
Serves 4

AMERICAN	IMPERIAL/METRIC
$\frac{1}{2}$ cup short cut macaroni	2 oz./50 g. short cut macaroni
1 cup grated Cheddar cheese	4 oz./100 g. Cheddar cheese, grated
2 eggs	2 eggs
seasoning	seasoning
little oil for frying	little oil for frying

Cook the pasta as previously directed, drain and refresh with cold water. Grate the cheese. In a basin beat the eggs together, season well and then stir in the macaroni and the cheese. Heat the oil in a frying pan and drop in tablespoons of the mixture. Fry until crisp and golden, turn over and cook the other side. Drain well and then serve with grilled tomatoes and peas, or a mixed salad.

Chicken with pineapple (see page 54)

Pasta brunch (see page 44)

CHEESE AND BACON NOODLES

Cooking time 15 minutes
Serves 4

AMERICAN	IMPERIAL/METRIC
½ lb. egg noodles	8 oz./225 g. egg noodles
½ lb. bacon slices	8 oz./225 g. lean streaky bacon
1 tablespoon oil	1 tablespoon oil
2 cups grated Cheddar cheese	8 oz./225 g. Cheddar cheese, grated
⅔ cup cultured sour cream	¼ pint/1½ dl. soured cream
black pepper	black pepper

Cook the noodles as previously directed. Meanwhile, remove the bacon rinds and cut the bacon into small pieces. Heat the oil and fry the bacon until crisp, then drain, but reserve 2 tablespoons of the bacon fat. Drain the noodles and rinse out the pan. Heat the bacon fat in the saucepan, return the noodles and toss lightly. Grate the cheese and add to the noodles, together with the soured cream and black pepper. Cook over very low heat until the ingredients are very hot, stirring occasionally. Arrange the noodles and cheese on a hot platter and sprinkle the crumbled bacon on top.

MACARONI AND EGGS LYONNAISE

Cooking time 25 minutes
Serves 4

AMERICAN	IMPERIAL/METRIC
6 tablespoons butter	3 oz./75 g. butter
½ lb. onions, sliced	8 oz./225 g. onions, sliced
6 tablespoons flour	1½ oz./40 g. flour
scant 2 cups milk	¾ pint/4 dl. milk
salt and freshly ground black pepper	salt and freshly ground black pepper
⅓ lb. short cut macaroni	6 oz./175 g. short cut macaroni
4 hard-cooked eggs, halved	4 hard-boiled eggs, halved
¾ cup grated cheese	3 oz./75 g. cheese, grated

Melt 2 oz. (50 g., ¼ cup) of the butter and fry the onion gently until softened and just turning colour. Remove from the heat and stir in the flour. Blend in the milk, bring up to simmering point, season to taste with salt and pepper and cook gently for 20 minutes. Meanwhile, cook the macaroni until just tender. Drain well and mix into the sauce. Season to taste. Cover the base of a warmed buttered ovenproof shallow dish with a layer of the macaroni mixture. Arrange the eggs cut side downwards and cover with the remaining macaroni in sauce. Sprinkle generously with grated cheese and dot with the remaining butter. Cook under the grill until golden brown and bubbling. Serve immediately with tossed green salad or buttered peas.

EGG NOODLE NESTS

Cooking time 30 minutes
Oven temperature 350°F., 180°C., Gas Mark 4
Serves 4

AMERICAN	IMPERIAL/METRIC
½ lb. egg noodles or egg vermicelli	8 oz./225 g. egg noodles or egg vermicelli
2 tablespoons butter	1 oz./25 g. butter
4 eggs, hard-cooked	4 eggs, hard-boiled
1¼ cups béchamel sauce (see page 13)	½ pint/3 dl. béchamel sauce (see page 13)
1 small can shrimp	1 small can prawns
1 teaspoon anchovy paste	1 teaspoon anchovy essence
parsley	parsley

Cook the egg noodles as previously directed, drain. Return to the pan with the butter, stir and then turn into a shallow ovenproof dish, making a border round the edge of the dish. Halve the eggs and arrange in the centre. Make up the sauce, drain the prawns, then stir into the sauce together with the anchovy essence. Coat the eggs with the sauce. Reheat in a moderate oven for 15 minutes. Chop the parsley and sprinkle over the hot dish.

EGG AND MACARONI GRILL

Cooking time 35 minutes
Oven temperature 375°F., 190°C., Gas Mark 5
Serves 4–6

AMERICAN	IMPERIAL/METRIC
6 eggs	6 eggs
1 cup button mushrooms	4 oz./100 g. button mushrooms
1 small onion	1 small onion
$\frac{1}{4}$ cup butter	2 oz./50 g. butter
6 tablespoons flour	$1\frac{1}{2}$ oz./40 g. flour
scant 2 cups milk	$\frac{3}{4}$ pint/4 dl. milk
seasoning	seasoning
2 cups short cut macaroni	8 oz./225 g. short cut macaroni
$\frac{1}{2}$ cup grated Cheddar cheese	2 oz./50 g. Cheddar cheese, grated
$\frac{1}{4}$ cup grated Parmesan cheese	1 oz./25 g. Parmesan cheese, grated

Hard-boil the eggs for 12 minutes, drain and cool in cold water. Slice the mushrooms and finely chop the onion. Melt the butter and sauté the prepared vegetables for 5 minutes, until tender but not coloured. Stir in the flour and cook for 2 minutes. Gradually stir in the milk and bring to the boil, stirring. Cook for 2 minutes, season the sauce well. Cook the macaroni as previously directed, drain. Grease an ovenproof dish and turn the drained macaroni into the dish. Shell the eggs and cut in half lengthwise. Arrange the eggs on the macaroni. Spoon the sauce over the eggs to cover completely. Grate the Cheddar cheese and mix with the grated Parmesan, sprinkle over the mushroom sauce. Reheat for 10 minutes in a moderately hot oven, then flash under a hot grill.

QUICK BEEF PAPRIKA

Cooking time 20–25 minutes
Serves 4

AMERICAN	IMPERIAL/METRIC
1 medium-sized onion	1 medium-sized onion
1 tablespoon oil	1 tablespoon oil
1 cup mushrooms	4 oz./100 g. mushrooms
1 tablespoon tomato paste	1 tablespoon tomato purée
1 tablespoon paprika	1 tablespoon paprika
1 14-oz. can stewed steak in gravy or 1 lb. stewed beef	1 14-oz./396-g. can stewed steak in gravy or 1 lb./450 g. stewed beef
$\frac{1}{2}$ lb. egg noodles or short cut macaroni	8 oz./225 g. egg noodles or short cut macaroni
2 tablespoons butter	1 oz./25 g. butter

Finely slice the onion and sauté in the oil for 3–4 minutes. Slice the mushrooms and add to the pan. Continue cooking until the vegetables are tender. Stir in the tomato purée and paprika and cook for 2–3 minutes before adding the meat. Reduce the heat and gently simmer for 10 minutes.

Cook the noodles as previously directed, drain and return to the pan together with the butter. Toss well, then arrange the noodles in a border around a heated dish and spoon the beef paprika into the centre.

SAVOURY FLAN

Cooking time 50 minutes
Oven temperature 350°F., 180°C., Gas Mark 4
Serves 4

AMERICAN	IMPERIAL/METRIC
$\frac{1}{3}$ lb. vermicelli	6 oz./175 g. vermicelli
1 tablespoon butter	$\frac{1}{2}$ oz./15 g. butter
2 large onions	2 large onions
4 slices bacon	4 rashers bacon
1 tablespoon oil	1 tablespoon oil
2 eggs plus milk to make up to $1\frac{1}{4}$ cups	2 eggs plus milk to make up to $\frac{1}{2}$ pint/3 dl.
salt, pepper and nutmeg	salt, pepper and nutmeg
4 tomatoes	4 tomatoes
watercress	watercress

Cook the vermicelli as previously directed, drain. Butter a deep ovenproof pie plate and press the vermicelli into the base and round the sides to form a lining. Thinly slice the onions and snip up the bacon then sauté in the oil until tender. Turn into the prepared dish. Beat the eggs and milk together, season well, add nutmeg to taste and strain over the onion and bacon. Skin the tomatoes, slice and arrange round the edge of the dish to prevent the pasta from crisping. Cook in a moderate oven for 35–40 minutes. Serve hot or cold, garnished with watercress.

Pork fillet and spaghetti with wine sauce (see page 59)

CHINATOWN MACARONI

Cooking time 35 minutes
Serves 4

AMERICAN	IMPERIAL/METRIC
¼ cup ground beef steak	2 oz./50 g. beef steak
¼ cup ground fresh pork	2 oz./50 g. fresh pork
⅓ cup diced salt pork	2 oz./50 g. salt pork
2 medium-sized onions	2 medium-sized onions
½ clove garlic	½ clove garlic
1 15-oz. can peeled plum tomatoes	1 15-oz./425-g. can peeled plum tomatoes
salt, pepper and cayenne pepper	salt, pepper and cayenne pepper
½ lb. short cut macaroni	8 oz./225 g. short cut macaroni

Put the beef and fresh pork through a mincer or ask the butcher to do it for you. Cut up the salt pork and heat in a frying pan until the fat is melted. Add the peeled chopped onions and fry until brown. Stir in the minced meat and brown slightly. Add the finely chopped garlic, tomatoes and seasoning and cayenne to taste. Simmer until tender, about ½ hour. Meanwhile cook the macaroni in boiling salted water until tender, then drain well. Pour the sauce over the macaroni and serve piping hot.

CONTINENTAL SAUSAGES

Cooking time 30 minutes
Serves 4

AMERICAN	IMPERIAL/METRIC
1 tablespoon oil	1 tablespoon oil
1 lb. pork sausage links	1 lb./450 g. pork sausages
4 medium-sized tomatoes	4 medium-sized tomatoes
1 clove garlic	1 clove garlic
2 teaspoons flour	2 teaspoons flour
⅔ cup bouillon or white wine	¼ pint/1½ dl. stock or white wine
2 teaspoons sugar	2 teaspoons sugar
seasoning	seasoning
½ lb. egg noodles or pasta spirals	8 oz./225 g. egg noodles or pasta spirals
½ cup grated cheese	2 oz./50 g. cheese, grated

Heat the oil and gently fry the sausages for 10 minutes, turning occasionally. Skin the tomatoes, remove the seeds and roughly chop the flesh. Crush the clove of garlic. Place the sausages on a dish and keep warm. Add the flour to the pan then gradually stir in the stock or wine, the tomatoes, garlic, sugar and seasoning. Simmer for 5 minutes. Return the sausages to the sauce and continue to simmer for a further 10 minutes.

Cook the noodles as previously directed, drain and turn onto a serving dish. Arrange the sausages on the pasta and pour the sauce over. Sprinkle the grated cheese over the sauce. Place under a hot grill until the cheese is golden and bubbly.

FRANKFURTER SAVOURY

Cooking time 20 minutes
Serves 4

AMERICAN	IMPERIAL/METRIC
3 stalks celery	3 stalks celery
1 large onion	1 large onion
3 tablespoons oil	2 tablespoons oil
1 can condensed tomato soup	1 can condensed tomato soup
½ can water	½ can water
1 lb. frankfurters or knackwurst	1 lb./450 g. frankfurters or knackwurst
½ lb. egg noodles or spaghetti	8 oz./225 g. egg noodles or spaghetti
2 tablespoons butter	1 oz./25 g. butter
1 tablespoon Worcestershire sauce	1 tablespoon Worcestershire sauce

Slice the celery and onion thinly and sauté in the oil for 3–4 minutes. Stir in the soup and water, bring to the boil and simmer for 2–3 minutes. Add the frankfurters or knackwurst, cover the pan and gently simmer for 10 minutes.

Cook the noodles as previously directed, drain. Return to the pan and toss in the butter. Place the noodles on a hot serving dish, arrange the frankfurters or knackwurst on top. Stir the Worcestershire sauce into the sauce then spoon it over the sausages.

Cooking time about 20 minutes
Serves 4

AMERICAN	IMPERIAL/METRIC
$\frac{3}{4}$ cup ground beef	6 oz./175 g. minced beef
$\frac{3}{4}$ cup ground pork	6 oz./175 g. minced pork
$\frac{1}{2}$ cup fresh bread crumbs soaked in milk	1 oz./25 g. fresh breadcrumbs soaked in milk
2 teaspoons chopped parsley	2 teaspoons chopped parsley
pinch grated lemon rind	pinch grated lemon rind
1 egg yolk	1 egg yolk
salt, pepper, onion salt	salt, pepper, onion salt
$2\frac{1}{2}$ cups beef bouillon	1 pint/6 dl. beef stock
$\frac{1}{2}$ lb. egg noodles or long spaghetti	8 oz./225 g. egg noodles or long spaghetti
2 tablespoons butter	1 oz./25 g. butter
poppy seeds	poppy seeds
6 tablespoons cream cheese	3 oz./75 g. cream cheese
1 tablespoon flour	1 tablespoon flour

Mix the meats together, add the soaked, squeezed bread, then the parsley, lemon rind, egg yolk and seasonings; the mixture should be soft. Shape into small meatballs and chill in the refrigerator. Heat the stock until simmering, drop in the meatballs and cook gently for 10–12 minutes. Remove and keep warm. Cook the egg noodles as previously directed, drain. Toss in butter, sprinkle with poppy seeds and keep warm.

Soften the cheese then beat in the flour. Gradually add a little of the stock, then add to the remainder in a pan, stir and bring to the boil. Add the meatballs and simmer for a further 2–3 minutes. Arrange the noodles in a border around a heated dish, then spoon the meatballs and sauce into the centre.

HAM TIMBALES

Cooking time 35 minutes
Oven temperature 375°F., 190°C., Gas Mark 5
Serves 6

AMERICAN	IMPERIAL/METRIC
$\frac{1}{2}$ cup short cut spaghetti or macaroni	2 oz./50 g. short cut spaghetti or macaroni
$\frac{1}{4}$ cup butter	2 oz./50 g. butter
6 tablespoons toasted bread crumbs	5 tablespoons toasted breadcrumbs
2 eggs	2 eggs
$\frac{1}{4}$ cup cultured sour cream	3 tablespoons soured cream
$\frac{1}{2}$ cup chopped cooked ham	4 oz./100 g. cooked ham
2 tablespoons chopped parsley	$1\frac{1}{2}$ tablespoons chopped parsley
black pepper and salt	black pepper and salt

Cook the pasta as previously directed. Butter the timbales (individual moulds or soufflé dishes approximately $\frac{1}{4}$ pint ($1\frac{1}{2}$ dl., $\frac{2}{3}$ cup) in capacity) and dust with the toasted breadcrumbs. Separate the eggs. Cream 1 oz. (25 g., 2 tablespoons) of the butter with a fork and gradually work in the egg yolk, then the soured cream, ham, finely chopped, and the parsley. Finally add the whisked egg whites and season with black pepper and a little salt. Add the cooked pasta. Turn into the prepared moulds, cover with the remaining breadcrumbs and then trickle over the remaining butter, melted. Bake in a moderately hot oven for 15–20 minutes. The timbales should be crisp on top and creamy inside. To serve, turn out onto hot plates and garnish with sprigs of parsley or leave in the soufflé dishes. Serve as a starter.

MACARONI CHEESE – NEW STYLE

Cooking time 20–25 minutes
Serves 4

AMERICAN	IMPERIAL/METRIC
1 cup short cut macaroni	4 oz./100 g. short cut macaroni
2 slices bacon	2 oz./50 g. streaky bacon
1 small onion	1 small onion
3 tablespoons butter	1½ oz./45 g. butter
6 tablespoons flour	1½ oz./45 g. flour
2½ cups milk	1 pint/6 dl. milk
salt and pepper	salt and pepper
pinch each cayenne and mustard	pinch each cayenne and mustard
1 cup grated Cheddar cheese	4 oz./100 g. Cheddar cheese, grated
¼ cup Parmesan cheese	1 oz./25 g. Parmesan cheese

Cook the macaroni as previously directed. De-rind the bacon and snip into small pieces. Cut the onion into thin rings. Melt the butter and sauté the bacon and onion for 2–3 minutes. Sprinkle over the flour, cook the roux, then gradually stir in the milk. Bring to the boil, add the seasonings, stirring all the time, and simmer for 3–4 minutes. Drain the macaroni well, then stir into the sauce. Mix the cheeses together and stir three-quarters into the sauce. Pour into an oval dish. Sprinkle over the remaining cheese then cook under a hot grill until golden and crispy.

SPAGHETTI PIZZA

Cooking time 30 minutes
Serves 4

AMERICAN	IMPERIAL/METRIC
½ lb. long spaghetti	8 oz./225 g. long spaghetti
1 cup grated Cheddar cheese	4 oz./100 g. Cheddar cheese, grated
2 eggs	2 eggs
seasoning	seasoning
¾ cup diced ham or salami	4 oz./100 g. ham or salami, diced
3 tablespoons oil	2 tablespoons oil
tomatoes	tomatoes

Cook the spaghetti as previously directed and drain well. Grate the cheese. In a large bowl beat the eggs then mix in the cheese, seasoning and diced meat. Add the spaghetti and mix well with the savoury egg, cheese and meat mixture. Heat the oil in a medium-sized frying pan and add the pizza mix. Cook gently until brown and set on the underside, about 5–8 minutes, then turn onto a plate and slide back into the pan to cook the second side. Turn out and garnish with tomato slices. Serve piping hot.

CRISPY NOODLES AND ONION RINGS

Cooking time 10 minutes
Serves 4

AMERICAN	IMPERIAL/METRIC
½ lb. short cut egg noodles	8 oz./225 g. short cut egg noodles
1–2 tablespoons olive oil	1–2 tablespoons olive oil
1 large Spanish onion	1 large Spanish onion
oil for frying	oil for frying
1¼ cups milk	½ pint/3 dl. milk
3 tablespoons flour	2 tablespoons flour
salt	salt

Cook the noodles until tender, drain well, return to the pan with 1–2 tablespoons olive oil and toss until coated to prevent them sticking together. Peel the onion, slice across and separate into rings. Put a frying basket in a deep pan half full with oil and heat to 380°F. (193°C.) or until a cube of bread will turn golden in 1 minute. Fry the cooked noodles, 2–3 tablespoons at a time, in the hot fat until crisp and golden. Drain on absorbent paper, sprinkle with salt and keep hot. Toss the onion rings, a few at a time, in milk and then in flour, and fry in the same way as the noodles. Drain on absorbent paper and season with salt. Mix the onion rings with the fried noodles and serve at once. Serve with grilled steak, pork or lamb chops, sausages, gammon or fried fillets of fish.

Illustrated on pages 56–7

SALADS

Pasta with salads or as a salad? It sounds a strange mixture to some people but is an ideal way of making a salad into a meal. The way the current prices of vegetables are rising I think that it is very important to make the very most of them. Green peppers, lettuce, cucumber, cauliflowers and mushrooms are all gradually becoming luxuries but with only small amounts of these salads can be made exciting and interesting.

Pasta shapes for salads must be cooked until firm but not too soft; the pasta is then refreshed by running under cold water in a colander. Allow to cool and then use with various sauces and dressings.

Salad making is a most creative process as one can use favourite vegetables to make attractive arrangements which take very little more time than throwing a few lettuce leaves with a tomato into a bowl. Crisp cabbage, cauliflower, chicory, grated carrots or thin carrot sticks, red cabbage, frozen or canned corn all add excitement and colour to salads. Remember only to dress the salad immediately before serving; sometimes it is more economical to serve the dressing separately so that remains can be stored in an airtight plastic box in the fridge for future use.

Food must have eye appeal and with salads it is so easy to arrange the ingredients in rings or pretty patterns and store until ready to eat. Cooked pasta stores well in the refrigerator and adds nourishment to the salad as well as helping to feed those with hearty appetites. Do give this idea a try as it is just as good for party meals as it is for using leftovers.

French dressing Mix one part oil to two parts vinegar (preferably wine vinegar) with seasoning. Crushed garlic, dried herbs or French mustard may be added for extra flavour. To make mayonnaise see page 11.

DEVILLED SALAD

Cooking time 10–12 minutes
Serves 4

AMERICAN	IMPERIAL/METRIC .
¾ cup lumachine shells or short cut macaroni	3 oz./75 g. lumachine shells or short cut macaroni
curry sauce (see page 13) or 3 tablespoons bottled chutney sauce	curry sauce (see page 13) or 2 tablespoons bottled chutney sauce
2 stalks celery	2 stalks celery
½ small green sweet pepper	½ small green pepper
½ cup mayonnaise	scant ¼ pint/1 dl. mayonnaise
1 tablespoon raisins	1 tablespoon raisins
3 tablespoons coffee cream	2 tablespoons single cream

Cook the pasta. When just tender, drain and refresh with cold water. Prepare the curry sauce. Dice the celery and green pepper finely. Turn the mayonnaise, curry sauce, raisins and cream into a bowl and mix well together; finally, add the cooked pasta and prepared vegetables. Toss well and then spoon into a salad bowl.

For a change add diced cooked chicken or turkey to this salad, and then sprinkle with toasted almonds.

PASTA AND CHICKEN SALAD

Cooking time 12 minutes
Serves 4

AMERICAN	IMPERIAL/METRIC
1 cup small pasta shells or rings	4 oz./100 g. small pasta shells or rings
$\frac{1}{3}$ cup olive oil	4 tablespoons olive oil
2 tablespoons lemon juice	1$\frac{1}{2}$ tablespoons lemon juice
seasoning	seasoning
pinch nutmeg	pinch nutmeg
1$\frac{1}{2}$ cups cooked diced chicken	8 oz./225 g. cooked diced chicken
$\frac{3}{4}$ cup cooked peas	4 oz./100 g. cooked peas
1 red sweet pepper, deseeded and cut into shreds	1 red pepper, deseeded and cut into shreds
1–2 stalks celery, sliced diagonally	1–2 stalks celery, sliced diagonally
lettuce or escarole	lettuce or escarole

Cook the pasta for about 12 minutes, then drain well and, while still hot, add the mixed oil and lemon juice and toss well together. Set aside to chill. When ready to serve, add seasoning, a pinch of nutmeg, chicken, peas, red pepper and celery. Arrange some leaves of lettuce round a salad bowl and pile the mixture in the centre.

HAM AND PINEAPPLE SALAD

Cooking time 10–12 minutes
Serves 4

AMERICAN	IMPERIAL/METRIC
$\frac{1}{2}$ cup short cut macaroni	2 oz./50 g. short cut macaroni
1 green sweet pepper	1 green pepper
2 stalks celery	2 stalks celery
$\frac{1}{4}$ cup mayonnaise	3 tablespoons mayonnaise
seasoning	seasoning
4 large slices ham	4 large slices ham
lettuce leaves	lettuce leaves
4 rings pineapple	4 rings pineapple
2 tomatoes	2 tomatoes
half bunch watercress	half bunch watercress

Cook the macaroni, drain, refresh with cold water and drain again. Chop the green pepper and celery into small dice, mix with the mayonnaise and seasoning and stir in the macaroni. Place a spoonful of the salad mixture on one half of each slice of ham, then fold the remaining half over. Serve on a bed of lettuce with a pineapple ring on each portion of ham and garnished with the tomatoes and watercress.

SUMMER WALDORF SALAD

Cooking time 10–12 minutes
Serves 4–6

AMERICAN	IMPERIAL/METRIC
$\frac{3}{4}$ cup spaghetti rings or short cut macaroni	3 oz./75 g. spaghetti rings or short cut macaroni
1 7-oz. can tuna fish	1 7-oz./198-g. can tuna fish
2 red apples	2 red apples
1 tablespoon lemon juice	1 tablespoon lemon juice
2 stalks celery	2 stalks celery
1 tablespoon raisins	1 tablespoon raisins
seasoning	seasoning
$\frac{1}{3}$ cup mayonnaise	4 tablespoons mayonnaise
1 tablespoon cultured sour cream	1 tablespoon soured cream
1 tablespoon walnuts	1 tablespoon walnuts

Cook the spaghetti rings, drain, refresh with cold water and drain again. Drain and flake the tuna fish. Core the apples and chop into rough pieces (do not remove the skins); toss in the lemon juice. Dice the celery. Turn the pasta into a large mixing bowl, add the flaked fish, apples, celery, raisins and seasoning. Fold in the mayonnaise and soured cream. Mix well and turn into a salad bowl. Roughly chop the walnuts and sprinkle over the salad.

MACARONI SALAD

Cooking time 10–12 minutes
Serves 4

AMERICAN	IMPERIAL/METRIC
1 cup elbow macaroni	4 oz./100 g. elbow macaroni
2 tablespoons lemon juice	1½ tablespoons lemon juice
1 tablespoon olive oil	1 tablespoon olive oil
3 tablespoons vinegar	2 tablespoons vinegar
3 tablespoons chopped chives or 1 teaspoon grated onion	2 tablespoons chopped chives or 1 teaspoon grated onion
3–4 stalks celery (with leaves if possible), diced	3–4 stalks celery (with leaves if possible), diced
¼ cup chopped parsley	3 tablespoons chopped parsley
3 tablespoons chopped canned pimiento	2 tablespoons chopped canned pimento
12 stuffed olives, chopped	12 stuffed olives, chopped
¼ cup cultured sour cream	3 tablespoons soured cream
salt and freshly ground pepper	salt and freshly ground pepper
lettuce or escarole	lettuce or escarole
1–2 tomatoes	1–2 tomatoes

Cook the macaroni until just tender – *al dente*. Mix the lemon juice, oil and vinegar well together. When the macaroni is cooked, drain well and while still hot, toss in the dressing, then set aside to cool. Mix all the other ingredients, except the lettuce and tomatoes, season with salt and freshly ground pepper. When ready to serve, mix with the macaroni and arrange on a bed of lettuce or escarole. Garnish with slices or wedges of tomato.

RUSSIAN SALAD

Cooking time 10–12 minutes
Serves 4

AMERICAN	IMPERIAL/METRIC
¾ cup spaghetti rings or short cut macaroni	3 oz./75 g. spaghetti rings or short cut macaroni
⅔ cup mayonnaise	¼ pint/1½ dl. mayonnaise
pepper and onion salt	pepper and onion salt
¾ cup diced cooked mixed vegetables	3 oz./75 g. cooked mixed vegetables, diced
chopped chives or scallions	chopped chives or spring onions

Cook the pasta and when just tender, drain and refresh with cold water. Spoon the mayonnaise into a bowl, add seasonings and then stir in the cooked pasta and mixed vegetables. Turn into a salad bowl and garnish with chives.

HAM SALAD

Cooking time 10 minutes
Serves 4–6

AMERICAN	IMPERIAL/METRIC
¾ cup lumachine shells or short cut macaroni	3 oz./75 g. lumachine shells or short cut macaroni
1 cup shredded ham	6 oz./175 g. ham
⅓ cup ripe olives	2 oz./50 g. black olives
2 teaspoons French mustard	2 teaspoons French mustard
⅔ cup mayonnaise	¼ pint/1½ dl. mayonnaise

Cook the pasta. When just tender, drain and refresh with cold water. Shred the ham and stone the olives. Stir the mustard into the mayonnaise and then add the shells, ham and olives. Toss well. Turn into a salad bowl.

PROVENCALE PASTA SALAD

Cooking time 12 minutes
Serves 4–6

AMERICAN	IMPERIAL/METRIC
½ lb. pasta wheels or shells	8 oz./225 g. pasta wheels or shells
salt	salt
1 clove garlic, crushed	1 clove garlic, crushed
⅔ cup French dressing	¼ pint/1½ dl. French dressing
1 crisp lettuce	1 crisp lettuce
3 hard-cooked eggs, halved	3 hard-boiled eggs, halved
⅔ cup mayonnaise	¼ pint/1½ dl. mayonnaise
6 anchovy fillets	6 anchovy fillets
1 7½-oz. can tuna fish	1 7½-oz./213-g. can tuna fish
2 ripe tomatoes	2 ripe tomatoes
1 small red or green sweet pepper	1 small red or green pepper
8 ripe olives	8 black olives
8 green stuffed olives	8 green stuffed olives

Cook the pasta wheels or shells in boiling salted water until just tender. Drain thoroughly. Add the garlic to the French dressing, moisten the pasta generously with the dressing and toss lightly until well covered. Leave to cool. Wash and dry the lettuce and line a large flat plate. Place the eggs, yolks upwards, in a line down the dish and top each one with mayonnaise and a twisted anchovy fillet. Arrange a line of prepared pasta on either side of the eggs. Flake up the tuna fish, dress it with mayonnaise and arrange it alongside one line of pasta. Finish with another line of pasta down the edge of the dish. Cut each tomato in six and the pepper into slices and arrange over the pasta. Garnish with black and stuffed green olives. Serve with crusty French bread.

Illustrated on page 61

MARYLAND SALAD

Cooking time 10 minutes
Serves 4

AMERICAN	IMPERIAL/METRIC
¾ cup mini shells or short cut macaroni	3 oz./75 g. mini shells or short cut macaroni
1 canned red pimiento	1 canned red pimento
⅔ cup canned corn	3 oz./75 g. canned sweetcorn
½ cup mayonnaise	scant ¼ pint/1 dl. mayonnaise
pepper and onion salt	pepper and onion salt
mustard and cress	mustard and cress

Cook the pasta. When just tender, drain and refresh with cold water. Chop the red pimento. Turn the sweetcorn into a bowl and add the mayonnaise and seasonings. Finally stir in the remaining ingredients and turn into a salad bowl. Garnish with little bunches of cress.

GARDEN SALAD

Cooking time 10 minutes
Serves 4–6

AMERICAN	IMPERIAL/METRIC
¾ cup short cut macaroni or mini shells	3 oz./75 g. short cut macaroni or mini shells
¼ cup French dressing	3 tablespoons French dressing
3 scallions	3 spring onions
1 small green sweet pepper	1 small green pepper
2 stalks celery	2 stalks celery
1¼ cups diced Swiss cheese	4 oz./100 g. Swiss cheese, diced
2 tomatoes	2 tomatoes
seasoning	seasoning
⅓ cup mayonnaise	4 tablespoons mayonnaise

Cook the macaroni, drain, refresh with cold water and drain again. Stir the French dressing into the macaroni, toss lightly and chill. Prepare the remaining ingredients: finely chop the spring onions, chop the green pepper and celery and dice the cheese. Cut the tomatoes into wedges for garnishing. Stir the prepared vegetables and cheese into the pasta together with the seasoning. Finally fold in the mayonnaise. Turn into a salad bowl and garnish with the tomato wedges.

ITALIAN SALAD

Cooking time 10–12 minutes
Serves 4

AMERICAN	IMPERIAL/METRIC
¾ cup lumachine shells or short cut macaroni	3 oz./75 g. lumachine shells or short cut macaroni
½ cup canned salata mixed vegetables	3 oz./75 g. canned salata mixed vegetables
½ cup canned crushed pineapple	3 oz./75 g. canned crushed pineapple
1 tablespoon currants	1 tablespoon currants
seasoning	seasoning
3 tablespoons French dressing	2 tablespoons French dressing

Cook the pasta and when just tender, drain and refresh with cold water. Chop the salata roughly and turn into a mixing bowl. Add the remaining ingredients and toss well. Turn into a salad bowl. Serve as part of an hors-d'oeuvre or with cold meats and other salad.

PRAWN CUCUMBER BOATS

Cooking time 10–12 minutes
Serves 4–6

AMERICAN	IMPERIAL/METRIC
2 cucumbers	1 large straight cucumber
seasoning	seasoning
½ cup pasta shells or spaghetti rings	2 oz./50 g. pasta shells or spaghetti rings
2 scallions	2 spring onions
⅓ cup shelled shrimp or prawns	2 oz./50 g. peeled prawns
¼ cup mayonnaise	3 tablespoons mayonnaise
dash Angostura bitters	dash Angostura bitters
1 teaspoon anchovy paste	1 teaspoon anchovy essence
⅔ cup fresh shrimp or prawns	¼ pint/1½ dl. fresh prawns
watercress or lettuce	watercress or lettuce

Cut the cucumber in half lengthwise. With a teaspoon scoop out the seeds, discard them and then scoop out a little more of the flesh and cut this into small dice. Sprinkle the hollowed skins with salt and turn upside down to drain. Cook the pasta and when just tender, drain and refresh with cold water. Mix the chopped cucumber and spring onions with the prawns. Add the mayonnaise and remaining ingredients except for the fresh prawns and watercress. Mix thoroughly. Wipe the cucumber skins with kitchen paper to remove salt and juices and then cut a sliver off the bottom of each to steady them. Set the 'boats' on an oval platter and fill with the salad mixture. Garnish with the fresh prawns and some watercress or lettuce. To serve, cut across into portions.

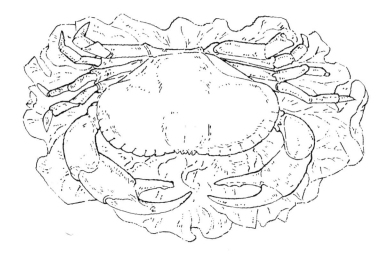

Cooking time 10 minutes
Serves 4

AMERICAN	IMPERIAL/METRIC
$\frac{1}{3}$ lb. pasta shells	6 oz./175 g. pasta shells
1 7-oz. can tuna fish or salmon	1 7-oz./198-g. can tuna fish or salmon
1 3$\frac{1}{4}$-oz. can crabmeat	1 3$\frac{1}{4}$-oz./92-g. can crabmeat
1 4-oz. can lobster (optional)	1 4-oz./113-g. can lobster (optional)
1 small onion or 6 scallions	1 small onion or 6 spring onions
1 small green sweet pepper	1 small green pepper
1 small red sweet pepper	1 small red pepper
6 olives (ripe or stuffed)	6 olives (black or stuffed)
anchovies (optional)	anchovies (optional)

Dressing

AMERICAN	IMPERIAL/METRIC
oil from can of tuna fish	oil from can of tuna fish
$\frac{2}{3}$ cup salad oil	$\frac{1}{4}$ pint/1$\frac{1}{2}$ dl. salad oil
$\frac{1}{4}$ cup wine vinegar	3 tablespoons wine vinegar
1–2 cloves garlic (according to taste)	1–2 cloves garlic (according to taste)
$\frac{1}{4}$ teaspoon fennel seed	$\frac{1}{4}$ teaspoon fennel seed
salt and pepper	salt and pepper

Cook the shells until firm but cooked, drain and rinse with cold water. Open the cans of fish and reserve the oil from the tuna fish. Chop the onions finely and cut the green and red peppers into strips or small dice. Halve and stone the olives. Mix the pasta shells with the peppers, olives, onions and flaked fish. Do not break up the fish too much. Make the dressing in a bowl by whisking the ingredients together (crush the garlic before whisking) or better still by mixing in the blender at top speed. Pour the dressing over the salad and mix well. Lay the anchovy fillets over the top and serve on a bed of lettuce, with halved spring onions and a side salad of sliced tomatoes sprinkled with dill and French dressing.

Illustrated on page 60

Cooking time 10–12 minutes
Serves 4–6

AMERICAN	IMPERIAL/METRIC
1$\frac{1}{2}$ cups pasta shells	6 oz./175 g. pasta shells
2 cups sliced mushrooms	8 oz./225 g. mushrooms, sliced
2 scallions, finely chopped	2 spring onions, finely chopped
1 small green sweet pepper, cut into strips	1 small green pepper, cut into strips
$\frac{1}{2}$ cucumber, diced	$\frac{1}{4}$ cucumber, diced
4 tomatoes	4 tomatoes
$\frac{1}{3}$ cup oil	4 tablespoons oil
1 tablespoon vinegar	1 tablespoon vinegar
salt and pepper	salt and pepper
1 bunch watercress	1 bunch watercress
1 apple, diced and mixed with 3 tablespoons lemon juice	1 apple, diced and mixed with 2 tablespoons lemon juice
about $\frac{3}{4}$ lb. cold meat or chicken	10–12 oz./300–350 g. cold meat or chicken

Marinade

AMERICAN	IMPERIAL/METRIC
3 tablespoons salad oil	2 tablespoons salad oil
$\frac{1}{2}$ teaspoon dry mustard	$\frac{1}{2}$ teaspoon dry mustard
1 clove garlic, crushed	1 clove garlic, crushed
scant 2 cups vinegar	$\frac{3}{4}$ pint/4 dl. vinegar
pinch mixed herbs	pinch mixed herbs

Cook the pasta shells, drain and rinse in cold water. Mix all the ingredients for the marinade together and pour over the sliced mushrooms and pasta shells. Allow to stand for at least 1 hour, turning the mixture over from time to time. Remove the mushrooms and pasta shells to the salad bowl and add the spring onions, green pepper, cucumber and tomatoes, cut into wedges. Make the remaining marinade into a dressing by adding the oil, vinegar and salt and pepper. Toss the salad in this dressing, arrange the watercress around the edge of the bowl, then make a ring of diced apple inside the watercress. Arrange the cold meat on a plate and serve with crispy French bread. Cold chicken, turkey, beef, lamb or ham mixed with salami make a tasty meal.

This recipe is not suitable for freezing.

COCKTAIL SALAD

Cooking time 10 minutes
Serves 4

AMERICAN	IMPERIAL/METRIC
¾ cup mini shells or short cut macaroni	3 oz./75 g. mini shells or short cut macaroni
2 stalks celery	2 stalks celery
1 canned red pimiento	1 canned red pimento
½ cup mayonnaise	scant ¼ pint/1 dl. mayonnaise
¼ cup tomato chutney	2 oz./50 g. tomato chutney
dash Angostura bitters	dash Angostura bitters
⅓ cup shelled shrimp	2 oz./50 g. peeled prawns

Cook the pasta. When just tender, drain and refresh with cold water. Dice the celery and chop the red pimento. Spoon the mayonnaise and tomato chutney into a bowl, mix, then stir in the remaining ingredients. Toss together and turn into a salad bowl.

COUNTRY SALAD

Cooking time 15 minutes
Serves 4

AMERICAN	IMPERIAL/METRIC
¾ cup mini pasta shells or spaghetti rings	3 oz./75 g. mini pasta shells or spaghetti rings
2 medium-sized tomatoes	2 medium-sized tomatoes
⅓ cup ripe olives	2 oz./50 g. black olives
1 cup button mushrooms	4 oz./100 g. button mushrooms
squeeze lemon juice	squeeze lemon juice
¼ cup French dressing	3 tablespoons French dressing
seasoning	seasoning

Cook the pasta. When just tender, drain and refresh with cold water. Skin the tomatoes, quarter and remove the seeds. Cut each quarter in half lengthwise. Stone the olives. Wash and trim the mushrooms, quarter and cook for 2–3 minutes in 2 tablespoons water and a squeeze of lemon juice. Cook quickly, uncovered, so that the liquid is well reduced by the time the mushrooms are cooked. Turn the mushrooms and their juice into a bowl, add the French dressing and then stir in the remaining ingredients. Season well and toss with a fork, then turn into a salad bowl.

PASTA SLAW

Cooking time 10–12 minutes
Serves 4

AMERICAN	IMPERIAL/METRIC
¾ cup spaghetti rings or short cut macaroni	3 oz./75 g. spaghetti rings or short cut macaroni
1 cup shredded white cabbage	3 oz./75 g. white cabbage
½ small green sweet pepper	½ small green pepper
1 small carrot	1 small carrot
1 tablespoon chopped chives	1 tablespoon chopped chives
½ cup mayonnaise	scant ¼ pint/1 dl. mayonnaise
1 tablespoon cultured sour cream	1 tablespoon soured cream
1 tablespoon vinegar	1 tablespoon vinegar
2 teaspoons sugar	2 teaspoons sugar
chopped parsley	chopped parsley

Cook the spaghetti rings. When just tender drain and refresh with cold water. Prepare the vegetables: finely shred the cabbage, dice the green pepper, grate the carrot and chop the chives. Spoon the mayonnaise into a bowl and add the soured cream, vinegar and sugar. Mix well together and then stir in the remaining prepared ingredients. Toss well, turn into a salad bowl and sprinkle with chopped parsley.

FISH

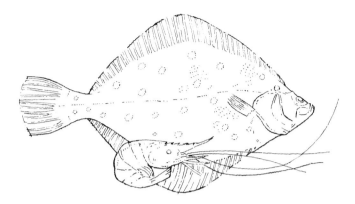

Fish and pasta make a perfect combination for many meals and here again is an ideal situation for the creative cook. Not only can you serve pasta in place of rice and potatoes with the more traditional fish recipes but exciting combinations of quick meals with canned fish are possible and delicious. I find that even resistant fish eaters can be brought round with pasta-fish combinations. For the more sophisticated, super dishes with garlic can add a new dimension to the menu.

Like everything else, fish is becoming more expensive and the addition of pasta means that it still feeds the family without straining the budget as you can allow less fish per portion and still provide a substantial and nourishing meal.

There are a few simple rules to remember when choosing fresh fish. Fish should never have an unpleasant smell if fresh. Look for bright eyes, red gills, firm flesh and a stiff tail. Frozen and canned fish are all ideal for use in pasta dishes as well as firm white fish and salmon. The more oily fishes, such as mackerel and herring, are not quite so suitable, I feel.

Small pasta shapes with tomato sauce are excellent to serve with small portions of fish or fish fingers for children instead of chipped potatoes.

BAKED FISH WITH PASTA SHELLS

Cooking time 45 minutes
Oven temperature 400°F., 200°C., Gas Mark 6
Serves 4

AMERICAN	IMPERIAL/METRIC
4 haddock or cod steaks	4 haddock or cod steaks
6 tablespoons butter	3 oz./75 g. butter
salt and pepper	salt and pepper
$\frac{1}{2}$ cup grated cheese	2 oz./50 g. cheese, grated
$\frac{3}{4}$ cup white wine or cider	generous $\frac{1}{4}$ pint/1$\frac{1}{2}$ dl. white wine or cider
2 tomatoes, halved	2 tomatoes, halved
$\frac{1}{3}$ lb. pasta shells	6 oz./175 g. pasta shells
2 teaspoons grated lemon rind	2 teaspoons grated lemon rind
1 tablespoon chopped parsley	1 tablespoon chopped parsley
parsley sprig for garnish	parsley sprig for garnish

Wash and trim the fish. Arrange in a buttered ovenproof dish. Season, cover with grated cheese and dot with butter. Pour in the wine or cider. Cover with greaseproof paper and bake in a moderately hot oven for 20 minutes. Remove the paper and add the tomato halves, season and dot with butter. Bake for a further 15 minutes or until the fish is cooked and a golden colour. Meanwhile cook the pasta shells until just tender. Drain. Melt 2 oz. (50 g., $\frac{1}{4}$ cup) butter in the pan, add the shells, lemon rind and chopped parsley and season well. Mix and just before serving spoon into the dish around the fish. Garnish with a sprig of parsley.
Illustrated on pages 24–5

MEDITERRANEAN FISH NOODLES

Cooking time 15–20 minutes
Serves 6

AMERICAN	IMPERIAL/METRIC
3 tablespoons olive oil	2 tablespoons olive oil
1 Spanish onion	1 Spanish onion
1 clove garlic, finely chopped	1 clove garlic, finely chopped
1 small red sweet pepper, chopped	1 small red pepper, chopped
1 small green sweet pepper, chopped	1 small green pepper, chopped
1 2-oz. can anchovies, chopped	1 2-oz./57-g. can anchovies, chopped
scant 2 cups sieved Italian plum tomatoes	$\frac{3}{4}$ pint/4 dl. sieved Italian plum tomatoes
$\frac{1}{4}$ teaspoon basil	$\frac{1}{4}$ teaspoon basil
$\frac{1}{2}$ teaspoon tarragon	$\frac{1}{2}$ teaspoon tarragon
4 cod fillets or steaks	4 cod fillets or steaks
freshly milled black pepper	freshly milled black pepper
1 lb. tagliatelle	1 lb./450 g. tagliatelle

Heat the oil in a heavy frying pan or stewpan. Add the onion, garlic, peppers and anchovies with the oil from the can. Sauté until all the vegetables are soft. Stir in the sieved tomatoes, basil, tarragon and small chunks of cod and season with freshly milled black pepper. Simmer in the pan, uncovered, until the fish is tender but not falling apart. While the fish is cooking, cook the tagliatelle in boiling salted water until tender. To serve, toss half the fish sauce with the noodles and spoon the remaining sauce on top.

This mixture can be mixed with the noodles and frozen in a polythene bag or box, or a shallow casserole. Reheat in a covered casserole in a moderate oven.

PASTA BRUNCH

Cooking time 15 minutes
Serves 4–6

AMERICAN	IMPERIAL/METRIC
$\frac{1}{2}$ lb. spaghetti	8 oz./225 g. spaghetti
salt	salt
$\frac{1}{4}$ cup butter	2 oz./50 g. butter
2 tablespoons chopped parsley	$1\frac{1}{2}$ tablespoons chopped parsley
freshly ground black pepper	freshly ground black pepper
$\frac{3}{4}$–1 lb. smoked haddock or cod fillet	12 oz.–1 lb./350–450 g. smoked haddock or cod fillet
lemon juice	lemon juice
3 eggs, beaten	3 eggs, beaten

Cook the spaghetti until just tender. Drain, then return to the hot pan with the butter and chopped parsley and season well with black pepper. Meanwhile, poach the smoked fish for 12–15 minutes, drain and flake and mix into the spaghetti. Sprinkle with lemon juice to taste. Turn the spaghetti and fish into a warm dish and stir in the beaten eggs. When thoroughly mixed, serve immediately with wooden pasta forks or salad servers to avoid mashing the spaghetti.

Illustrated on page 29

SALMON KEDGEREE

Cooking time 15 minutes
Serves 4

AMERICAN	IMPERIAL/METRIC
$1\frac{1}{2}$ cups pasta shells	6 oz./175 g. pasta shells
2 eggs	2 eggs
1 7-oz. can salmon	1 7-oz./198-g. can salmon
$\frac{1}{4}$ cup butter	2 oz./50 g. butter
seasoning	seasoning
1 tablespoon chopped parsley	1 tablespoon chopped parsley
little diced cucumber	little diced cucumber

Cook the pasta shells, drain. Hard-boil the eggs, rinse well in cold water, remove the shells and chop finely. Drain the salmon, reserving the juice, remove the skin and bones then flake the fish.

Turn the shells back into the pan together with the butter, seasoning, parsley, salmon and juice and the eggs, reserving a little chopped egg to garnish. Gently reheat, stirring occasionally. Turn into a heated dish and garnish with diced cucumber and the remaining egg.

CREAMED SALMON

Cooking time 20 minutes
Serves 4

AMERICAN	IMPERIAL/METRIC
1 cup lumachine shells	4 oz./100 g. lumachine shells
3 stalks celery	3 stalks celery
1⅓ cups canned pink salmon	8 oz./225 g. canned pink salmon
3 tablespoons butter	1½ oz./40 g. butter
6 tablespoons flour	1½ oz./40 g. flour
scant 2 cups milk	¾ pint/4 dl. milk
¼ cup cream	3 tablespoons cream
salt, pepper and onion salt	salt, pepper and onion salt
1 teaspoon anchovy paste	1 teaspoon anchovy essence
2 teaspoons lemon juice	2 teaspoons lemon juice
1 teaspoon tomato paste	1 teaspoon tomato purée
⅓ cup grated Cheddar cheese	1½ oz./40 g. Cheddar cheese, grated
1 can red pimientos	1 can red pimentos
2 slices toast	2 slices toast

Cook the pasta shells, drain, refresh with cold water and drain again. Cut the celery into small strips and blanch by plunging into boiling water for 5 minutes; refresh.

Drain the salmon, reserving the juice, remove bones and skin and flake the fish. Melt the butter, add the flour and cook the roux. Gradually add the milk and salmon juice and continue to stir until thickened. Add the cream, seasonings and flavourings and simmer for 2 minutes.

Stir in the celery, grated cheese, salmon and cooked pasta. Gently reheat and garnish with the red pimentos cut in slices. Serve with triangles of crisp toast.

GOLDEN HADDOCK GRILL

Cooking time 30 minutes
Serves 6

AMERICAN	IMPERIAL/METRIC
1 lb. smoked haddock fillet	1 lb./450 g. smoked haddock fillet
¼ lb. egg noodles	4 oz./100 g. egg noodles
1 small package frozen peas	1 small packet frozen peas
6 tablespoons butter	3 oz./75 g. butter
½ cup flour	2 oz./50 g. flour
1¼ cups milk	½ pint/3 dl. milk
black pepper and nutmeg	black pepper and nutmeg
¾ cup fresh bread crumbs	1½ oz./40 g. fresh breadcrumbs
4 tomatoes	4 tomatoes

Place the fish in a large frying pan, cover with cold water, bring to the boil and poach gently for 5–8 minutes. Drain the fish, reserving ¼ pint (1½ dl., ⅔ cup) of the liquor in a jug. Cook the noodles for 5 minutes then add the peas and continue to cook for a further 5 minutes; drain. Rinse out the saucepan. Melt 2 oz. (50 g., ¼ cup) of the butter, add the flour and cook until a roux is formed. Add the reserved fish liquor then gradually stir in the milk. Bring to the boil, stirring, and simmer for 2 minutes to make a sauce. Flake the fish and remove any bones and skin. Add the fish to the sauce, together with the noodles and peas. Season with pepper and nutmeg. Pour into a round ovenproof dish. Sprinkle with the breadcrumbs and dot with the remaining butter. Place under a hot grill together with the tomatoes, cut in half. Grill for about 4 minutes until golden brown.

MEDITERRANEAN SPAGHETTI

Cooking time 15–20 minutes
Serves 4

AMERICAN	IMPERIAL/METRIC
2 onions	2 onions
3 tablespoons oil	2 tablespoons oil
1 clove garlic	1 clove garlic
1 5-oz. can artichoke hearts	1 5-oz./142-g. can artichoke hearts
1¼ cups milk	½ pint/3 dl. milk
1½ cups grated Gruyère cheese	6 oz./175 g. Gruyère cheese, grated
seasoning	seasoning
½ lb. spaghetti	8 oz./225 g. spaghetti
1 7½-oz. can crabmeat	1 7½-oz./213-g. can crabmeat
⅓ cup sherry	4 tablespoons sherry
1 tablespoon chopped parsley	1 tablespoon chopped parsley

Finely slice the onions and sauté in the oil until tender but not coloured. Crush the garlic and drain the artichoke hearts then cut each in half. Add the milk, cheese, garlic, artichokes and seasoning to the onions. Cook slowly until the cheese melts. Cook the spaghetti. Meanwhile add the flaked crabmeat and sherry to the cheese sauce, reheat for a few minutes. Drain the spaghetti and mix together with the sauce. Turn into a heated dish and sprinkle with the parsley.

SEAFOOD SUPPER

Cooking time 15–20 minutes
Oven temperature 350°F., 180°C., Gas Mark 4
Serves 4

AMERICAN	IMPERIAL/METRIC
8 fillets flounder or sole	8 fillets plaice
½ cup butter	4 oz./100 g. butter
scant 2 cups milk	¾ pint/4 dl. milk
salt and black pepper	salt and black pepper
2 cups lumachine shells	8 oz./225 g. lumachine shells
½ cup flour	2 oz./50 g. flour
⅔ cup coffee cream	¼ pint/1½ dl. single cream
⅓ cup sherry	4 tablespoons sherry
⅓ cup shelled shrimp	2 oz./50 g. peeled prawns
2 tomatoes	2 tomatoes
1 lemon	1 lemon

Roll the fillets of plaice round small knobs of butter, using 2 oz. (50 g., ¼ cup) of the butter. Place the fillets in a greased ovenproof dish with ¼ pint (1½ dl., ⅔ cup) of the milk and season well. Cook in the oven for 10–12 minutes. Cook the pasta shells. Meanwhile make a sauce by melting the rest of the butter in a saucepan, then adding the flour and gradually stirring in the remaining milk and the milk drained from the poached fish. Bring to the boil and stir for a further 2 minutes until cooked; finally add the cream, sherry and prawns. Season and simmer gently. Drain the pasta and turn onto a heated dish. Top with the poached fillets and coat with the cream and prawn sauce. Cut the tomato into slices and the lemon into wedges and use to garnish the dish.

Cooking time 45–50 minutes
Serves 4–6

AMERICAN	IMPERIAL/METRIC
$\frac{1}{3}$ cup olive oil	4 tablespoons olive oil
1 large onion, sliced	1 large onion, sliced
2 cloves garlic, finely chopped	2 cloves garlic, finely chopped
1 1 lb. 13-oz. can plum tomatoes	1 1 lb. 13-oz./822-g. can plum tomatoes
$1\frac{1}{2}$ teaspoons salt	$1\frac{1}{2}$ teaspoons salt
1 small red sweet pepper	1 small red pepper
1 teaspoon basil	1 teaspoon basil
1 cup cooked green peas	5 oz./150 g. cooked green peas
1 lb. filleted white fish, cooked and flaked	1 lb./450 g. filleted white fish, cooked and flaked
1 lb. spaghetti	1 lb./450 g. spaghetti

Heat the olive oil in a saucepan; sauté the onion and garlic for 10 minutes, stirring frequently. Add the tomatoes, salt, red pepper cut into strips and basil. Bring to the boil, cover and cook over a low heat for 30 minutes. Add the peas and fish. Cook for 10 minutes, stirring occasionally. Cook and drain the spaghetti and heap on a serving platter. Taste the sauce for seasoning, pour over the spaghetti, toss lightly and serve immediately.

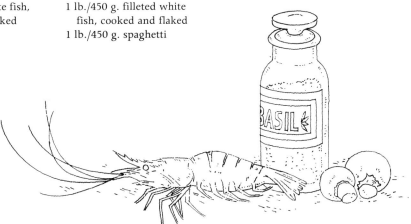

Cooking time 50 minutes
Serves 4

AMERICAN	IMPERIAL/METRIC
2 shallots	2 shallots
bouquet garni	bouquet garni
scant cup sherry	7 fl. oz./2 dl. sherry
$\frac{1}{2}$ cup butter	4 oz./100 g. butter
$\frac{1}{4}$ cup flour	1 oz./25 g. flour
scant 2 cups bouillon	$\frac{3}{4}$ pint/4 dl. stock
1 cup button mushrooms	4 oz./100 g. button mushrooms
1 clove garlic	1 clove garlic
2 teaspoons tomato paste	2 teaspoons tomato purée
seasoning	seasoning
2 tomatoes	2 tomatoes
1 lb. scampi	1 lb./450 g. scampi
seasoned flour	seasoned flour
3 tablespoons cream	2 tablespoons cream
chopped parsley	chopped parsley
2 cups lumachine shells	8 oz./225 g. lumachine shells

Chop the shallots and simmer with the bouquet garni in the sherry until it is reduced by half. Remove the herbs. Melt 1 oz. (25 g., 2 tablespoons) of the butter, add the flour, stir well and allow to colour. Stir in the stock, bring up to the boil then add the mushrooms, the crushed garlic, tomato purée and seasoning. Cover and simmer gently for 20 minutes. Skin the tomatoes, cut each into eight pieces and remove the seeds. Add the shallots, sherry and tomatoes to the sauce and simmer for a further 15 minutes. Roll the scampi in seasoned flour and sauté for 5 minutes in 2 oz. (50 g., $\frac{1}{4}$ cup) of the butter, then add to the sauce. Stir in the cream then spoon the sauce into a heated dish; cover and keep warm. Cook the pasta shells, drain and return to the hot saucepan, together with the remaining butter and the chopped parsley. Toss and then arrange around the shellfish.

Cooking time 15 minutes
Serves 4–6

AMERICAN	IMPERIAL/METRIC
$\frac{1}{2}$ lb. vermicelli or fine noodles	8 oz./225 g. vermicelli or fine noodles
3 onions, chopped	3 onions, chopped
2 cloves garlic, finely chopped	2 cloves garlic, finely chopped
$\frac{1}{4}$ cup ground nuts	1 oz./25 g. ground nuts
2 teaspoons salt	2 teaspoons salt
$\frac{1}{2}$ teaspoon dried ground chili peppers	$\frac{1}{2}$ teaspoon dried ground chilli peppers
$\frac{1}{4}$ teaspoon saffron	$\frac{1}{4}$ teaspoon saffron
$\frac{1}{2}$ teaspoon grated lemon rind	$\frac{1}{2}$ teaspoon grated lemon rind
2 teaspoons anchovy paste	2 teaspoons anchovy paste
$\frac{1}{4}$ cup oil	3 tablespoons oil
$1\frac{1}{2}$ lb. raw shrimp, shelled and deveined	$1\frac{1}{2}$ lb./675 g. raw shrimps, shelled and deveined
1 cup finely shredded coconut	3 oz./75 g. finely grated coconut
scant 2 cups milk	$\frac{3}{4}$ pint/4 dl. milk

Cook and drain the vermicelli and keep warm. Pound together the onions, garlic, nuts, salt, chilli peppers, saffron, lemon rind and anchovy paste. Heat the oil in a frying pan and sauté the mixture for 3 minutes, stirring almost constantly. Add the shrimps, mix well and sauté for 2 minutes. Add the coconut and milk; bring to the boil and cook over low heat for 1 minute. Serve on the vermicelli.

MUSSELS WITH SPAGHETTI

Cooking time 25 minutes
Serves 4

AMERICAN	IMPERIAL/METRIC
$2\frac{1}{2}$ quarts mussels	4 pints/$2\frac{1}{4}$ litres mussels
$\frac{1}{2}$ lb. spaghetti	8 oz./225 g. spaghetti
$\frac{1}{4}$ cup butter	2 oz./50 g. butter
1 large onion	1 large onion
2 cloves garlic	2 cloves garlic
$\frac{2}{3}$ cup white wine	$\frac{1}{4}$ pint/$1\frac{1}{2}$ dl. white wine
salt and pepper	salt and pepper
squeeze lemon juice	squeeze lemon juice
3 tablespoons chopped parsley	2 tablespoons chopped parsley

Scrub the mussels in clean salt water and remove the beards – discard any which are open and do not close when tapped. Rinse thoroughly. Cook the spaghetti in boiling salted water. Heat half the butter in a large frying pan. Chop the onions and garlic and sauté gently without browning. Add the mussels to the pan and shake gently over the heat until they open. Add the wine and shake gently. Cook for about 15 minutes. Meanwhile drain the spaghetti, toss in the remaining butter and shake over freshly ground black pepper. Arrange on individual plates. Remove some of the mussels from the shells and lay in the centre, surround the plates with mussels in their shells for garnish, pour a little wine sauce over each portion and sprinkle with parsley.

Illustrated opposite

Mussels with spaghetti

POULTRY

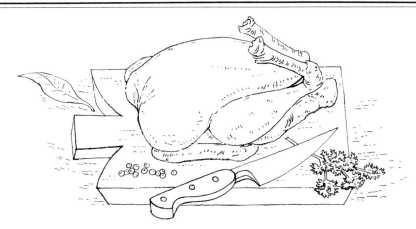

Chicken, turkey and duck combine splendidly with pasta, both hot and cold. Chicken is still relatively inexpensive and a small one can make anything from soup through to the main course, with a snack meal thrown in from the leftovers.

As chicken meat and pasta are fairly bland try serving a spicy sauce. Fruit-flavoured bases such as pineapple also make interesting combinations with pasta and poultry.

Delicious salads with small pasta shapes can be made by cutting either cubes or thin slices of poultry. Thinly sliced duck with fresh sliced orange, lettuce, watercress, walnuts and rings or small shells is delicious. Cubes of chicken mixed with curried mayonnaise served with any small shapes and garnished with lemon twists and rings of green pepper is another delicious and easy salad.

Chicken can be used in fillings for lasagne and cannelloni and in spaghetti sauces. The combinations are limitless for creating one's own favourite recipes.

CHICKEN-NOODLE BAKE

Cooking time 35–45 minutes
Oven temperature 350°F., 180°C., Gas Mark 4
Serves 6

AMERICAN	IMPERIAL/METRIC
$\frac{1}{3}$ lb. fettuccine	6 oz./175 g. fettuccine
1 10-oz. package frozen mixed vegetables in butter sauce	1 10-oz./283-g. packet frozen mixed vegetables in butter sauce
1 10$\frac{1}{2}$-oz. can condensed cream of celery soup	1 10$\frac{1}{2}$-oz./298-g. can condensed cream of celery soup
1 10$\frac{1}{2}$-oz. can condensed cream of asparagus soup	1 10$\frac{1}{2}$-oz./298-g. can condensed cream of asparagus soup
1 cup milk	scant $\frac{1}{2}$ pint/2$\frac{1}{2}$ dl. milk
$\frac{1}{2}$ teaspoon salt	$\frac{1}{2}$ teaspoon salt
$\frac{1}{4}$ teaspoon pepper	$\frac{1}{4}$ teaspoon pepper
$\frac{1}{4}$ teaspoon dill weed	$\frac{1}{4}$ teaspoon dill weed
2 cups cooked diced chicken or turkey	12 oz./350 g. cooked diced chicken or turkey
$\frac{1}{4}$ cup cornflake crumbs	1 oz./25 g. cornflake crumbs

Cook and drain the noodles. Cook the vegetables according to the directions on the packet. Blend the soups, milk and seasonings in a 2-quart (2$\frac{1}{4}$-litre, 2$\frac{1}{2}$-quart) casserole. Stir in the chicken, noodles and mixed vegetables in butter sauce. Top with cornflake crumbs. Bake in a moderate oven for 20–30 minutes. This is a good way to use leftover chicken or turkey.

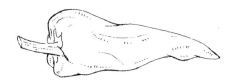

CHICKEN MAJORCA

Cooking time 50 minutes
Serves 4

AMERICAN	IMPERIAL/METRIC
$\frac{1}{4}$ cup oil	3 tablespoons oil
4 chicken pieces	4 chicken joints
1 Spanish onion	1 Spanish onion
$\frac{1}{4}$ cup flour	1 oz./25 g. flour
$2\frac{1}{2}$ cups chicken bouillon	1 pint/6 dl. chicken stock
seasoning	seasoning
pinch mixed herbs	pinch mixed herbs
3 oranges	3 oranges
1 can red pimientos	1 can red pimentos
6 stuffed olives	6 stuffed olives
$\frac{1}{2}$ lb. tagliatelle or egg noodles	8 oz./225 g. tagliatelle or egg noodles
6 tablespoons butter	3 oz./75 g. butter
2 tablespoons sugar	1 oz./25 g. castor sugar

Heat the oil and brown the chicken on both sides, then remove from the pan. Finely slice the onion, add to the pan and sauté for 3–4 minutes. Stir in the flour, cook for 2 minutes, then gradually add the stock. Bring to the boil, stirring, then replace the chicken and add seasoning and herbs. Cover the pan and gently simmer for 30–35 minutes. Grate the rind and squeeze the juice from one of the oranges. Stir both into the chicken. Carefully remove all peel from the remaining oranges and cut down into slices. Shred the pimentos into strips and slice the olives. Cook the pasta. Add the pimento and olives to the chicken. Melt 2 oz. (50 g., $\frac{1}{4}$ cup) of the butter in a frying pan. Sprinkle the orange slices with sugar and cook in the hot butter, turning once, until they begin to colour.

Drain the pasta when cooked and toss in the remaining butter. Arrange at one end of a heated platter. Place the chicken joints at the other end of the dish and coat with the orange and pimento sauce. Finally garnish with the glazed orange slices.

CHICKEN FORESTIERE

Cooking time 40–50 minutes
Oven temperature 400°F., 200°C., Gas Mark 6
Serves 4

AMERICAN	IMPERIAL/METRIC
4 chicken pieces	4 chicken joints
$\frac{1}{2}$ cup butter	4 oz./100 g. butter
8 slices bacon	8 rashers bacon
2 cups button mushrooms	8 oz./225 g. button mushrooms
seasoning	seasoning
6 tablespoons flour	$1\frac{1}{2}$ oz./40 g. flour
$1\frac{1}{4}$ cups chicken bouillon	$\frac{1}{2}$ pint/3 dl. chicken stock
$\frac{1}{2}$ lb. tagliatelle verdi or egg noodles	8 oz./225 g. tagliatelle verdi or egg noodles
$\frac{1}{3}$ cup cream	4 tablespoons cream

Cut the chicken joints in half, remove the skins, spread with 2 oz. (50 g., $\frac{1}{4}$ cup) of the butter and place each piece centrally on a trimmed bacon rasher. Chop the mushrooms, reserve half; sprinkle some on top of each chicken piece and season. Wrap the chicken up in the bacon. Place the wrapped chicken pieces on a buttered ovenproof dish, sprinkle with the remaining mushrooms and dot with 1 oz. (25 g., 2 tablespoons) butter. Cover and bake in a moderately hot oven for 30–40 minutes, until the chicken is tender. Drain off the liquor, re-cover the chicken and keep warm in a low oven.

Melt the remaining butter in a small saucepan, add the flour and cook for 2 minutes. Gradually stir in the hot chicken juices and then the stock. Simmer gently for 5 minutes. Cook and drain the tagliatelle, return to the pan with an extra knob of butter and cover. Gradually add the cream to the chicken sauce and check seasoning. Arrange the noodles in a border around a serving dish. Fill the centre with the chicken portions and coat with the mushroom and cream sauce.

Cannelloni (see page 18)

Mexican casserole (see page 68)

Cooking time 30 minutes
Oven temperature 400°F., 200°C., Gas Mark 6
Serves 4

AMERICAN	IMPERIAL/METRIC
1 14-oz. can pineapple chunks	1 14-oz./396-g. can pineapple chunks
4 chicken pieces	4 chicken joints
1 green sweet pepper	1 green pepper
$\frac{1}{2}$ lb. egg noodles	8 oz./225 g. egg noodles
1 tablespoon butter	$\frac{1}{2}$ oz./15 g. butter
freshly milled pepper	freshly milled pepper
grated nutmeg	grated nutmeg
1 teaspoon cornstarch	1 teaspoon cornflour
Marinade	
$\frac{2}{3}$ cup yogurt	$\frac{1}{4}$ pint/1$\frac{1}{2}$ dl. yogurt
1 clove garlic	1 clove garlic
3 tablespoons lemon juice	2 tablespoons lemon juice
3 tablespoons tomato paste	2 tablespoons tomato purée
$\frac{1}{2}$ teaspoon Tabasco	$\frac{1}{2}$ teaspoon Tabasco
$\frac{1}{2}$ teaspoon turmeric	$\frac{1}{2}$ teaspoon turmeric
$\frac{1}{2}$ teaspoon coriander	$\frac{1}{2}$ teaspoon coriander
$\frac{1}{4}$ teaspoon salt	$\frac{1}{4}$ teaspoon salt

Illustrated on page 28

Drain the can of pineapple, retaining the juice for the marinade. Make up the marinade by mixing all the ingredients with the pineapple juice. Put the chicken, with or without the skin as preferred, in a shallow dish or polythene bag and pour over the marinade. Leave the chicken in the marinade overnight or for several hours. (Chicken pieces can be frozen in the marinade.) Remove from the marinade, but do not scrape this from the chicken, which is then roasted in a moderately hot oven for 30 minutes. Meanwhile chop the green pepper into thin slices, having first removed the seeds. Blanch by placing in boiling water and allowing the water to return to the boil; drain well. Cook the noodles in boiling salted water for about 9–10 minutes. Drain, return to the saucepan with a knob of melted butter and sprinkle with freshly milled pepper and grated nutmeg.

Blend the cornflour with a little water and add the marinade. Heat with the pineapple chunks and green pepper and pour some over each portion of chicken; serve the remaining sauce separately.

CHICKEN A LA MAISON

Cooking time 1$\frac{3}{4}$ hours
Serves 4

AMERICAN	IMPERIAL/METRIC
1 3-lb. chicken	1 3-lb./1$\frac{1}{4}$-kg. chicken
1 medium-sized onion	1 medium-sized onion
1 carrot	1 carrot
1 stalk celery	1 stalk celery
seasoning	seasoning
3$\frac{3}{4}$ cups cold water	1$\frac{1}{2}$ pints/scant litre cold water
7 tablespoons butter	3$\frac{1}{2}$ oz./90 g. butter
6 tablespoons flour	1$\frac{1}{2}$ oz./40 g. flour
pinch nutmeg and ginger	pinch nutmeg and ginger
$\frac{1}{2}$ lb. tagliatelle or egg noodles	8 oz./225 g. tagliatelle or egg noodles
1 cup mushrooms	4 oz./100 g. mushrooms
1 4-oz. can Danish pâté	1 4-oz./113-g. can Danish pâté
$\frac{1}{4}$ cup cream	3 tablespoons cream
1 tablespoon chopped parsley	1 tablespoon chopped parsley

Rinse out the chicken and place in a saucepan together with the vegetables, roughly chopped, the seasoning and water. Bring to the boil, cover and simmer gently for 1–1$\frac{1}{4}$ hours, until the chicken is tender. Remove the chicken, cut into four portions, keep warm.

Melt 1$\frac{1}{2}$ oz. (40 g., 3 tablespoons) of the butter, add the flour and cook for 2 minutes. Strain the chicken stock and gradually add 1 pint (6 dl., 2$\frac{1}{2}$ cups) of it to make the sauce. Season well, add nutmeg and ginger.

Cook the pasta. Slice the mushrooms and sauté in 1 oz. (25 g., 2 tablespoons) of the butter, then add to the sauce and continue to simmer gently. Soften the pâté with a fork and gradually work in the cream; when the mixture is soft stir it into the sauce. Drain the pasta when cooked and toss in the remaining butter then arrange around the chicken. Coat in the pâté sauce. Sprinkle parsley over the dish.

CHICKEN AND BACON TETRAZZINI

Cooking time 40–45 minutes
Oven temperature 375°F., 190°C., Gas Mark 5
Serves 5–6

AMERICAN	IMPERIAL/METRIC
$\frac{1}{3}$ lb. long spaghetti	6 oz./175 g. long spaghetti
$\frac{1}{2}$ lb. Canadian bacon	8 oz./225 g. collar bacon
1 cup chopped cooked chicken	6 oz./175 g. cooked chicken
1 7-oz. can red sweet peppers	1 7-oz./198-g. can red sweet peppers
$\frac{3}{4}$ cup grated Cheddar cheese	3 oz./75 g. Cheddar cheese, grated
3 tablespoons butter	$1\frac{1}{2}$ oz./40 g. butter
6 tablespoons flour	$1\frac{1}{2}$ oz./40 g. flour
$\frac{2}{3}$ cup milk	$\frac{1}{4}$ pint/1$\frac{1}{2}$ dl. milk
2 cups chicken bouillon	$\frac{3}{4}$ pint/4 dl. chicken stock
salt and pepper	salt and pepper
$\frac{1}{4}$ teaspoon nutmeg	$\frac{1}{4}$ teaspoon nutmeg
3 tablespoons sherry	2 tablespoons sherry
1 egg yolk	1 egg yolk
$\frac{1}{4}$ cup flaked almonds	1 oz./25 g. flaked almonds

Break the spaghetti into 4-inch (10-cm.) lengths, cook and drain. Cut the bacon into $\frac{1}{2}$-inch (1-cm.) pieces and fry gently in a large pan until crisp but not brown. Cut the chicken into bite-sized pieces. Drain the can of peppers and slice them. Grate the cheese finely. Add the chicken and peppers to the bacon and cook for another 5 minutes. Stir in the cooked drained spaghetti, remove from the heat. Make a roux with the butter and flour, cook well then slowly add the milk and stock. Bring to the boil, stirring, and allow the sauce to thicken. Add the cheese. Season to taste and add the nutmeg and sherry. Stir in the egg yolk off the heat. Place the chicken mixture in an ovenproof dish, coat with the sauce and sprinkle with flaked almonds. Heat through for about 25 minutes in a moderately hot oven before serving.

CHICKEN SIMLA

Cooking time 30 minutes
Serves 4

AMERICAN	IMPERIAL/METRIC
1 Spanish onion	1 Spanish onion
6 tablespoons butter	3 oz./75 g. butter
1 tablespoon curry powder	1 tablespoon curry powder
$\frac{1}{2}$ cup flour	2 oz./50 g. flour
$2\frac{1}{2}$ cups chicken bouillon	1 pint/6 dl. chicken stock
pinch cayenne pepper	pinch cayenne pepper
$\frac{1}{8}$ teaspoon ground ginger	$\frac{1}{8}$ teaspoon ground ginger
3 tablespoons mango chutney	2 tablespoons mango chutney
2 cups chopped cooked chicken	12 oz./350 g. cooked chicken
$\frac{1}{2}$ lb. pasta spirals with egg or egg noodles	8 oz./225 g. pasta spirals with egg or egg noodles
3 tablespoons seedless white raisins	2 tablespoon sultanas
$\frac{2}{3}$ cup cultured sour cream	$\frac{1}{4}$ pint/1$\frac{1}{2}$ dl. soured cream

Finely chop the onion. Melt 2 oz. (50 g., $\frac{1}{4}$ cup) of the butter and sauté the onion until soft. Stir in the curry powder and flour and cook for 1 minute. Gradually blend in the stock, bring to the boil, then add the cayenne and ginger. Chop the mango chutney and stir it into the sauce. Continue simmering for 15 minutes.

Dice or shred the chicken. Cook the pasta. Add the chicken and sultanas to the sauce and simmer gently for a further 5 minutes, then stir in the soured cream and remove from the heat.

Drain the pasta and add the remaining butter; toss the pasta to melt the butter. Arrange the pasta in a heated dish and spoon over the chicken.

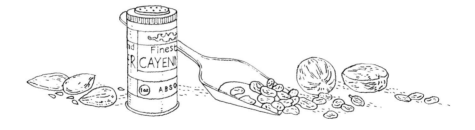

Crispy noodles and onion rings (see page 35)

CHICKEN PRINCESS

Cooking time 45 minutes
Serves 4

AMERICAN	IMPERIAL/METRIC
3 tablespoons butter	1½ oz./40 g. butter
4 small chicken pieces	4 small chicken joints
1 onion	1 onion
¼ cup flour	1 oz./25 g. flour
¼ teaspoon curry powder	¼ teaspoon curry powder
1¼ cups chicken bouillon	½ pint/3 dl. chicken stock
lemon juice	lemon juice
seasoning	seasoning
½ lb. pasta spirals with egg	8 oz./225 g. pasta spirals with egg
¼ cup cream	3 tablespoons cream
1 small can cut asparagus or ¼ lb. green beans	1 small can cut asparagus or 4 oz./100 g. green beans

Heat the butter and sauté the chicken joints until the meat has slightly stiffened but not coloured. Remove from the pan. Slice the onion and stir into the butter, cover and cook very gently for 5 minutes. Return the chicken to the pan, sprinkle on the flour and curry powder and then gradually add the stock, lemon juice and seasonings. Cover the pan and simmer gently until the chicken is tender. Meanwhile, cook the pasta spirals, drain and return to the pan with a knob of butter; cover with a lid. (The chicken may now be removed from the bone if preferred.) Stir the cream into the chicken, check seasonings and fold in the asparagus or cooked beans. Turn the pasta into a dish and spoon over the chicken.

COUNTRY CHICKEN CASSEROLE

Cooking time 45 minutes
Serves 4

AMERICAN	IMPERIAL/METRIC
⅓ cup oil	4 tablespoons oil
4 chicken pieces	4 chicken joints
seasoned flour	seasoned flour
4 carrots	4 carrots
2 onions	2 onions
1 clove garlic	1 clove garlic
pinch salt	pinch salt
2½ cups bouillon	1 pint/6 dl. stock
¼ lb. egg noodles	4 oz./100 g. egg noodles
1 cup mushrooms	4 oz./100 g. mushrooms
small package frozen peas	small packet frozen peas

Heat the oil in a large pan. Toss the chicken joints in seasoned flour and gently fry in the hot oil. Prepare and chop the carrots and onions. Crush the garlic clove with a pinch of salt and add with the vegetables to the golden brown chicken. Add the stock and bring to the boil. Cover and simmer for 15 minutes. Toss in the egg noodles, re-cover and continue cooking gently for 10 minutes. Remove the lid and add the sliced mushrooms and the peas. Cook for a further 5 minutes. Serve immediately.

CHICKEN LASAGNE

Cooking time 50 minutes
Oven temperature 400°F., 200°C., Gas Mark 6
Serves 4

AMERICAN	IMPERIAL/METRIC
3 oz. lasagne	3 oz./75 g. lasagne
1 cup chopped cooked chicken	6 oz./175 g. cooked chicken
3 tablespoons butter	1½ oz./40 g. butter
6 tablespoons flour	1½ oz./40 g. flour
1¼ cups chicken bouillon	½ pint/3 dl. chicken stock
⅔ cup milk	¼ pint/1½ dl. milk
seasoning	seasoning
pinch nutmeg	pinch nutmeg
squeeze lemon juice	squeeze lemon juice
toasted bread crumbs	toasted breadcrumbs
melted butter	melted butter

Cook the lasagne in plenty of boiling salted water for 12–14 minutes. Drain, rinse in cold water, drain well again. Chop the chicken. Make a sauce with the butter, flour, stock and milk. Season well with salt and pepper, add a pinch of nutmeg and a squeeze of lemon juice. Grease a 6-inch (15-cm.) square dish and line with a layer of lasagne. Put a layer of half the chicken on top and cover with a layer of sauce. Follow with another layer of lasagne, the remainder of the chicken and another layer of sauce. Top with a final layer of lasagne and rest of the sauce. Sprinkle with breadcrumbs and a little melted butter. Bake in a hot oven for 35 minutes.

MEAT DISHES

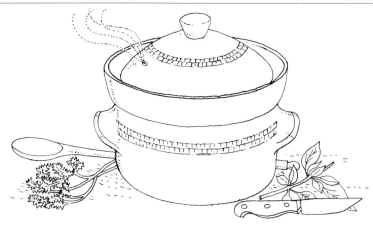

Meat dishes with pasta are of course an ideal combination and what better way to help out the family budget without serving dull, uninteresting meals? With cheaper cuts of meat made into delicious stews and casseroles the various pasta shapes make a superb accompaniment. The sauce of a casserole clings well to some of the different shapes, e.g., spirals or shells, so do experiment as you will find that the variations add infinite variety to your menus. Save yourself peeling potatoes by serving noodles with goulash or spirals with almost any kind of casserole. Leftover joints can be chopped finely or minced for a number of pasta dishes and the family will never even realise they are eating leftovers.

If you have a freezer make up several portions of bolognese or tomato sauce, sweet and sour sauce with pork, etc., and you will always have a large choice of meals to hand.

For a really continental-style meal serve a little pasta with or without sauce as a starter, then serve a joint with freshly cooked green vegetables.

PORK FILLET AND SPAGHETTI WITH WINE SAUCE

Cooking time 20 minutes

Serves 4

AMERICAN	IMPERIAL/METRIC
8 large prunes	8 large prunes
$1\frac{1}{4}$ cups red wine	$\frac{1}{2}$ pint/3 dl. red wine
$1\frac{1}{4}$ lb. pork tenderloin	$1\frac{1}{4}$ lb./600 g. pork fillet
3 tablespoons seasoned flour	2 tablespoons seasoned flour
7 tablespoons butter	$3\frac{1}{2}$ oz./90 g. butter
$\frac{1}{2}$ lb. spaghetti	8 oz./225 g. spaghetti
1 tablespoon chopped chives	1 tablespoon chopped chives
salt	salt
freshly ground black pepper	freshly ground black pepper
$\frac{2}{3}$ cup whipping cream	$\frac{1}{4}$ pint/$1\frac{1}{2}$ dl. double cream
1 tablespoon red currant jelly	1 tablespoon redcurrant jelly
lemon juice	lemon juice

Soak the prunes in the red wine for at least 4 hours or overnight. Then cook very gently in the red wine whilst preparing and cooking the meat. Trim the pork fillet and cut across into slices about $\frac{1}{2}$ inch (1 cm.) thick. Toss in seasoned flour and fry briskly in 2 oz. (50 g., $\frac{1}{4}$ cup) hot butter until browned on both sides. Lower the heat and spoon off the excess butter, then add $\frac{1}{4}$ pint (3 dl., $\frac{2}{3}$ cup) of the wine from the prunes. Cover and cook for 15 minutes or until the meat is tender. Meanwhile, cook the spaghetti, drain thoroughly and return to the pan with the remaining butter and the chives. Mix and season well. Keep warm. Blend 2 tablespoons of the wine sauce with the cream and stir this back into the pan. Cook until smooth and glossy. Add the redcurrant jelly, lemon juice and seasoning to taste. Add the prunes and pour over the spaghetti.

Illustrated on page 32

Tuna fish salad (see page 41)

Provençale pasta salad (see page 39)

PAPRIKA SCHNITZEL

Cooking time 15 minutes
Serves 4

AMERICAN	IMPERIAL/METRIC
1 lb. pork tenderloin or veal escalopes	1 lb./450 g. pork fillet or veal escalopes
1 clove garlic	1 clove garlic
3 tablespoons seasoned flour	2 tablespoons seasoned flour
6 tablespoons butter	3 oz./75 g. butter
1 red pimiento	1 red pimento
2 teaspoons paprika	2 teaspoons paprika
$1\frac{1}{4}$ cups coffee cream	$\frac{1}{2}$ pint/3 dl. single cream
$\frac{1}{2}$ lb. egg noodles or tagliatelle	8 oz./225 g. egg noodles or tagliatelle

Slice the pork fillet in half lengthwise and then cut each slice in half. Beat well until thin. Cut the clove of garlic and rub over the pork slices, then coat them in seasoned flour. Melt 2 oz. (50 g., $\frac{1}{4}$ cup) of the butter in a sauté pan and cook the pork until golden on both sides, about 6 minutes; remove the meat from the pan. Shred the red pimento and add to the pan together with the remaining flour and the paprika pepper. Cook for about 2 minutes. Remove from the heat and gradually stir in the cream. Return to the heat, stirring, and gently bring back to the boil. Add the pork and continue to cook very gently for a further 5–6 minutes.

Cook the noodles as previously directed. Drain the noodles and toss in the remaining butter. Turn the noodles onto each end of a heated dish and arrange the Schnitzel and sauce in the centre. Sprinkle with chopped parsley.

PORK CHOP SUEY

Cooking time 15 minutes
Serves 4

AMERICAN	IMPERIAL/METRIC
$\frac{1}{4}$ lb. egg noodles	4 oz./100 g. egg noodles
$\frac{3}{4}$ lb. pork tenderloin	12 oz./350 g. pork fillet
4 stalks celery	4 stalks celery
1 Spanish onion	1 Spanish onion
3 cups shredded crisp cabbage	8 oz./225 g. crisp cabbage
3 tablespoons oil	2 tablespoons oil
1 tablespoon soy sauce	1 tablespoon soy sauce
scant 2 cups chicken bouillon	$\frac{3}{4}$ pint/4 dl. chicken stock
1 16-oz. can bean sprouts	1 16-oz./453-g. can bean sprouts
seasoning	seasoning
1 tablespoon cornstarch	1 tablespoon cornflour
3 scallions	3 spring onions

Cook the noodles as previously directed, drain and refresh with cold water. Cut the meat into matchstick strips. Finely shred the celery, onion and cabbage. Heat the oil and when it is very hot add the meat and sauté for 1 minute. Stir in the prepared vegetables, fry for a further minute, then add the soy sauce and most of the chicken stock. Boil, stirring constantly, for another minute. Lower the heat, cover and continue to cook for 5 minutes. Add the bean sprouts, cooked noodles and seasoning and stir so that the vegetables are well mixed. Blend the cornflour with the remaining stock, add to the chop suey, return to the boil, stirring, and cook for a further minute. Turn into a heated bowl and garnish with strips of spring onion over the top.

PORK AMERICANA

Cooking time 30 minutes
Serves 4

AMERICAN	IMPERIAL/METRIC
1 lb. pork tenderloin	1 lb./450 g. pork fillet
1 large onion	1 large onion
1 green sweet pepper	1 green pepper
¼ cup oil	3 tablespoons oil
2 teaspoons curry powder	2 teaspoons curry powder
3 tablespoons brown sugar	2 tablespoons brown sugar
3 tablespoons onion chutney	2 tablespoons onion chutney
seasoning	seasoning
½ lb. pasta twistetti or grill shapes	8 oz./225 g. pasta twistetti or grill shapes
1 8-oz. can corn	1 8-oz./226-g. can sweetcorn
2 tablespoons butter	1 oz./25 g. butter
1 tablespoon chopped parsley	1 tablespoon chopped parsley

Cut up the pork into bite-sized pieces. Slice the onion and pepper. Heat the oil and stir in the meat, allow to colour. Add the vegetables and cook slowly until they are tender. Push the meat and vegetables to one side of the pan. Add the curry powder, brown sugar and chutney, mix well and allow this mixture to cook for 2–3 minutes before stirring it into the pork. Season, then cover the pan and continue to cook very gently for 12–15 minutes. Cook the pasta as previously directed. Stir the sweetcorn into the pork and gently reheat. Drain the pasta, toss in the butter and turn onto a heated dish. Pile the pork on top and garnish with the parsley.

NORMANDY PORK CHOPS

Cooking time 30 minutes
Serves 4

AMERICAN	IMPERIAL/METRIC
4 pork chops	4 pork chops
salt and black pepper	salt and black pepper
½ lb. egg noodles	8 oz./225 g. egg noodles
2 cups mushrooms	8 oz./225 g. mushrooms
6 tablespoons butter	3 oz./75 g. butter
¼ cup flour	1 oz./25 g. flour
1¼ cups dry cider	½ pint/3 dl. dry cider
pinch marjoram	pinch marjoram
⅔ cup coffee cream	¼ pint/1½ dl. single cream

Season the pork chops with salt and pepper and cook under a medium preheated grill for 20 minutes, turning once. When crisp and brown place on a serving dish and keep warm. Save the pan juices. Cook the noodles as previously directed.

Meanwhile, slice the mushrooms and sauté in 2 oz. (50 g., ¼ cup) of the butter. After 5 minutes add the flour and cook for a minute. Blend in the juice from the chops, together with the cider and marjoram. Simmer for 2 minutes, stirring all the time. Add the cream and reheat gently, but do not boil. Drain the noodles and toss in the remaining butter. Arrange the noodles around the chops and pour over the cider and cream sauce.

Apricot dessert (see page 71)

FLORENTINE HAM

Cooking time 20 minutes
Serves 4

AMERICAN	IMPERIAL/METRIC
4 thick slices ham or Canadian bacon	4 gammon rashers
3 tablespoons brown sugar	2 tablespoons brown sugar
few cloves	few cloves
½ lb. egg noodles	8 oz./225 g. egg noodles
1 8-oz. package frozen spinach	1 8-oz./226-g. packet frozen spinach
4 slices pineapple	4 slices pineapple
¼ cup butter	2 oz./50 g. butter
salt and black pepper	salt and black pepper
1 tablespoon cream	1 tablespoon cream

Snip the outside edge of each gammon rasher and then sprinkle with brown sugar. Stud with cloves and place under a hot grill for 4 minutes. Cook the noodles as previously directed. Cook the spinach according to the packet instructions.

Turn the gammon, grill for a further 4 minutes, then add the slices of pineapple and cook until golden. Drain the noodles and toss in 1 oz. (25 g., 2 tablespoons) of the butter, sprinkle with pepper. Drain the spinach well and return it to the pan together with the rest of the butter and the cream. Season well. Serve the gammon on top of the noodles on a heated dish. Fill the pineapple centres with spinach.

CHILLI CON CARNE

Cooking time 1½ hours
Serves 4

AMERICAN	IMPERIAL/METRIC
½ lb. chuck steak	8 oz./225 g. chuck steak
½ lb. lean shoulder pork	8 oz./225 g. lean shoulder pork
1 Spanish onion	1 Spanish onion
1 clove garlic	1 clove garlic
3 tablespoons oil	2 tablespoons oil
scant 2 cups beef bouillon	¾ pint/4 dl. beef stock
2 teaspoons tomato paste	2 teaspoons tomato purée
chili powder to taste	chilli powder to taste
1 tablespoon flour	1 tablespoon flour
1 bay leaf	1 bay leaf
pinch oregano	pinch oregano
seasoning	seasoning
½ lb. egg noodles	8 oz./225 g. egg noodles
1 8-oz. can red kidney beans	1 8-oz./226-g. can red kidney beans

Coarsely mince the beef and pork, then the onion. Crush the garlic. Heat the oil and brown the meats, onion and garlic, stirring occasionally. Add the stock and stir in the tomato purée, bring to the boil, cover and simmer gently for 1 hour. Blend the chilli powder and the flour together with a little cold water and add to the meat, together with the herbs and seasoning. Continue simmering for a further 15–20 minutes. Cook the noodles as previously directed.

Drain the kidney beans, then stir into the meats. Reheat. Drain the noodles and arrange in a border around a heated dish. Spoon the chilli con carne into the centre.

BEEF ITALIENNE

Cooking time about 30 minutes

Serves 4

AMERICAN	IMPERIAL/METRIC
1 medium-sized onion	1 medium-sized onion
1 small green sweet pepper	1 small green pepper
3 tablespoons butter	1½ oz./40 g. butter
¾ lb. beef round steak	12 oz./350 g. rump steak
½ cup mushrooms	2 oz./50 g. mushrooms
¼ cup flour	1 oz./25 g. flour
2½ cups beef bouillon	1 pint/6 dl. beef stock
3 tablespoons tomato paste	2 tablespoons tomato purée
seasoning, including black pepper	seasoning, including black pepper
⅓ lb. pasta spirals with egg	6 oz./175 g. pasta spirals with egg
3 tablespoons cultured sour cream	2 tablespoons soured cream

Finely chop the onion and shred the pepper, then sauté in the butter. Cut the beef into fingers and add with the sliced mushrooms to the vegetables. Sauté to seal and brown the meat. Add the flour, cook, then stir in the stock, tomato purée and seasoning. Simmer gently for 20–25 minutes until the beef is tender. Cook the pasta spirals as previously directed, drain, add a knob of butter and black pepper and turn into a dish. Stir the soured cream into the beef and spoon over the pasta.

BEEF AND MACARONI PIE

Cooking time 40 minutes

Oven temperature 400°F., 200°C., Gas Mark 6

Serves 4–6

AMERICAN	IMPERIAL/METRIC
1 cup short cut macaroni	4 oz./100 g. short cut macaroni
1 15½-oz. can minced beef with gravy	1 15½-oz./440-g. can minced beef with gravy
3 tablespoons tomato ketchup	2 tablespoons tomato ketchup
seasoning	seasoning
2–3 slices bread and butter	2–3 slices bread and butter

Cook the macaroni in plenty of boiling, salted water for 8 minutes, until tender; drain and return to the pan. Stir the minced beef into the macaroni, together with the ketchup and seasoning. Turn into a greased shallow ovenproof dish and top with sufficient buttered bread to cover; arrange the slices buttered side up. Bake in a moderately hot oven for 30 minutes until the bread is golden and crispy. Serve with crisp green vegetables.

GREEK MACARONI

Cooking time about 1 hour

Oven temperature 350°F., 180°C., Gas Mark 4

Serves 4

AMERICAN	IMPERIAL/METRIC
2 large onions	2 large onions
3 tablespoons oil	2 tablespoons oil
1 lb. ground beef	1 lb./450 g. minced beef
1 8-oz. can tomatoes	1 8-oz./226-g. can tomatoes
½ teaspoon cinnamon	½ teaspoon cinnamon
¼ teaspoon nutmeg	¼ teaspoon nutmeg
salt and black pepper	salt and black pepper
1½ cups short cut macaroni	6 oz./175 g. short cut macaroni
½ cup grated Parmesan cheese	6 tablespoons grated Parmesan cheese
3 eggs	3 eggs
⅔ cup coffee cream	¼ pint/1½ dl. single cream

Thinly slice the onions and sauté in the oil until tender but not coloured. Add the minced beef and brown well. Stir in the tomatoes and the seasonings. Simmer gently for about 20 minutes until the tomato juices have evaporated. Cook the macaroni as previously directed, drain and add to the seasoned meat mixture, together with about half the Parmesan cheese. Turn into a deep ovenproof dish. Beat the eggs well together, season and add the remaining cheese and the cream. Pour this over the meat mixture and bake in a moderate oven for about 35 minutes, until golden and crisp on top.

Cooking time about $1\frac{1}{4}$ hours
Serves 4

AMERICAN	IMPERIAL/METRIC
1 $1\frac{1}{4}$-lb. piece beef top round	1 $1\frac{1}{4}$-lb./550-g. piece topside
1 small onion	1 small onion
$\frac{1}{4}$ cup butter	2 oz./50 g. butter
1 tablespoon chopped parsley	1 tablespoon chopped parsley
3 tablespoons capers	2 tablespoons capers
6 tablespoons seasoned flour	$1\frac{1}{2}$ oz./40 g. seasoned flour
1 tablespoon oil	1 tablespoon oil
2 cups beef bouillon	$\frac{3}{4}$ pint/4 dl. beef stock
$\frac{1}{2}$ lb. egg noodles	8 oz./225 g. egg noodles
1 teaspoon vinegar	1 teaspoon vinegar
$\frac{2}{3}$ cup whipping cream	$\frac{1}{4}$ pint/$1\frac{1}{2}$ dl. double cream
seasoning	seasoning

Cut the topside into thin slices and then beat each piece until very thin. Grate the onion. Heat 1 oz. (25 g., 2 tablespoons) of the butter and sauté the onion, half the parsley and the capers for 3 minutes. Spread this mixture on the beef slices and roll up and tie, as for a parcel. Coat the rolls in the seasoned flour. Heat the oil, then seal the roulades and allow them to colour. Sprinkle on the remaining flour and cook gently, allowing to colour lightly. Stir in the stock, bring to the boil, cover the pan and gently simmer for $1-1\frac{1}{4}$ hours, until the beef is tender. Cook the noodles as previously directed.

Remove the roulades from the sauce and carefully cut away the string. Arrange the roulades on a heated dish and keep warm. Rapidly boil the sauce, then add the vinegar, reduce the heat and stir in the cream and seasoning. Drain the noodles and toss in the remaining butter. Arrange around the roulades and then coat both with the sauce. Sprinkle with the remaining parsley.

SPAGHETTI WITH SPICED MEATBALLS

Cooking time 20 minutes
Serves 4

AMERICAN	IMPERIAL/METRIC
1 lb. ground beef	1 lb./450 g. minced beef
1 onion, chopped	1 onion, chopped
1 cup soft bread crumbs	2 oz./50 g. fresh breadcrumbs
3 tablespoons tomato ketchup	2 tablespoons tomato ketchup
2 eggs, lightly beaten	2 eggs, lightly beaten
pinch cinnamon	pinch cinnamon
pinch ground cloves	pinch ground cloves
pinch nutmeg	pinch nutmeg
$\frac{3}{4}$ teaspoon salt	$\frac{3}{4}$ teaspoon salt
$\frac{1}{4}$ teaspoon pepper	$\frac{1}{4}$ teaspoon pepper
3 tablespoons olive oil	2 tablespoons olive oil
1 clove garlic, finely chopped	1 clove garlic, finely chopped
1 8-oz. can tomato sauce	1 8-oz./226-g. can tomato sauce
1 cup water	scant $\frac{1}{2}$ pint/2 dl. water
2 stalks celery, chopped	2 stalks celery, chopped
1 lb. thin spaghetti	1 lb./450 g. thin spaghetti
$\frac{1}{2}$ cup grated Parmesan cheese	2 oz./50 g. Parmesan cheese, grated

Mix together the beef, onion, breadcrumbs, ketchup, eggs, cinnamon, cloves, nutmeg, salt and pepper. Shape into 1-inch ($2\frac{1}{2}$-cm.) balls. Heat the oil in a pan and brown the meatballs and garlic. Add the tomato sauce, water and celery; cook over a low heat for 15 minutes. Cook the spaghetti and drain well. Pour the meatballs and sauce over the spaghetti and sprinkle with grated Parmesan cheese.

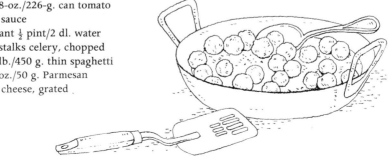

SWEDISH BEEF

Cooking time 1–1¼ hours
Serves 4

AMERICAN	IMPERIAL/METRIC
1 lb. chuck steak	1 lb./450 g. chuck steak
2 medium-sized onions	2 medium-sized onions
⅓ cup butter	2½ oz./65 g. butter
2½ cups beef bouillon	1 pint/6 dl. beef stock
grated lemon rind	grated lemon rind
pinch nutmeg	pinch nutmeg
salt and pepper	salt and pepper
1 red pimiento	1 red pimento
1 tablespoon chopped parsley	1 tablespoon chopped parsley
6 tablespoons cream cheese	3 oz./75 g. cream cheese
¼ cup flour	1 oz./25 g. flour
little extra bouillon	little extra stock
½ lb. pasta spirals or twistetti	8 oz./225 g. pasta spirals or twistetti
poppy seeds	poppy seeds

Cut the beef into thin strips, about 3 inches (7½ cm.) long. Finely slice the onions. Heat 1½ oz. (40 g., 3 tablespoons) of the butter, add the prepared beef and onions and sauté over brisk heat to colour and stiffen the meat. Stir in the stock and all flavourings. Cover and gently simmer for ¾–1 hour, until the meat is almost tender. Shred the pimento into thin fingers. Stir the pimento and parsley into the meat. Soften the cream cheese with a fork and gradually work in the flour and about 2 tablespoons cold stock until a smooth cream is made. Gradually stir this creamed mixture into the meat and continue simmering very gently for a further 10 minutes. Cook the pasta as previously directed, drain and toss in the remaining butter and 1 tablespoon poppy seeds. Turn the noodles onto a heated platter, then spoon the Swedish beef into the centre.

MEXICAN CASSEROLE

Cooking time 2 hours
Oven temperature 350°F., 180°C., Gas Mark 4
Serves 4–6

AMERICAN	IMPERIAL/METRIC
1 lb. beef stew meat	1 lb./450 g. stewing steak
3 tablespoons seasoned flour	2 tablespoons seasoned flour
3 tablespoons oil	2 tablespoons oil
1 large onion	1 large onion
1 carrot	1 carrot
1 7-oz. can peeled plum tomatoes	1 7-oz./198-g. can peeled plum tomatoes
¼ teaspoon chili powder	¼ teaspoon chilli powder
salt and pepper	salt and pepper
1¼ cups bouillon	½ pint/3 dl. stock
bouquet garni	bouquet garni
1 10-oz. can red kidney beans	1 10-oz./283-g. can red kidney beans
⅓–½ lb. pasta spirals	6–8 oz./175–225 g. pasta spirals

Preheat the oven. Cut the steak into small cubes, toss in seasoned flour and fry in the oil until nicely browned. Remove to a casserole dish. Chop the onion and carrot into small dice and fry gently for a few minutes, then add to the meat. Stir in the remaining flour, then add the tomatoes, chilli powder, seasoning, stock and bouquet garni. Cook for 1½ hours. When cooked, remove from the oven, take out the bouquet garni and taste for seasoning. Open the kidney beans, drain and add to the casserole. Replace the casserole in the oven for 20–30 minutes and cook the pasta spirals to accompany the casserole.

Illustrated on page 53

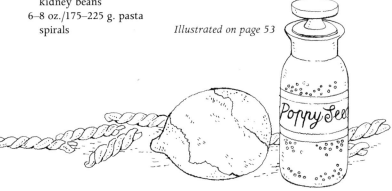

PUDDINGS & DESSERTS

Macaroni pudding has long been a nursery favourite in this country where we tend to feed a growing family with milk puddings. Pasta is ideal for children so introduce them early enough and it quickly becomes a favourite. It is a nourishing dish to offer at lunch or supper time. Babies usually love it and it is one of the easiest solid meals to introduce with savoury or sweet mixtures such as some of the fruit purées or milk pudding recipes given here.

It is interesting to have a few pasta puddings in your repertoire, but on the whole I think the texture of pasta is such that it blends better with savoury sauces.

APPLE AND RAISIN LASAGNE

Cooking time 40 minutes
Oven temperature 350°F., 180°C., Gas Mark 4
Serves 4

AMERICAN	IMPERIAL/METRIC
2 oz. lasagne	2 oz./50 g. lasagne
4 cooking apples	1 lb./450 g. cooking apples
$\frac{1}{4}$ cup sugar, or more to taste	2 oz./50 g. sugar, or more to taste
3 tablespoons water	2 tablespoons water
pinch cinnamon	pinch cinnamon
scant 2 cups custard or 1 15-oz. can custard	$\frac{3}{4}$ pint/4 dl. custard or 1 15-oz./425-g. can custard
3 tablespoons raisins	1 oz./25 g. raisins
$\frac{1}{4}$ cup walnuts	1 oz./25 g. walnuts

Cook the lasagne as previously directed and drain well. Refresh with cold water and drain again. Peel, core and dice the apples. Gently cook with the sugar, water and cinnamon in a covered pan until just tender. Make the custard. Grease a pie dish and line with lasagne. Add half the apples and raisins and 2 tablespoons of the custard. Cover with lasagne and the remainder of the apples and raisins and another 2 tablespoons of the custard. Top with the remaining lasagne and cover with the rest of the custard. Smooth over the top. Chop the walnuts and sprinkle over the pudding. Bake in a moderate oven for 20 minutes. Serve hot. Mincemeat may be used instead of the apple and raisin mixture if you prefer.

APRICOT PUDDING

Cooking time 30 minutes
Serves 4–6

AMERICAN	IMPERIAL/METRIC
3 cups milk	1¼ pints/¾ litre milk
¾ cup mini pasta shells	3 oz./75 g. mini pasta shells
1 small can apricots	1 small can apricots
¼ cup granulated sugar	2 oz./50 g. castor sugar
2 tablespoons gelatin	½ oz./15 g. gelatine
whipped cream and candied angelica leaves	whipped cream and angelica

Heat the milk. When simmering, add the mini pasta shells to the milk, stir and cook gently for 20 minutes; cool. Drain the apricots, reserving the juice. Chop the fruit and add with the sugar to the pudding. Place the gelatine and fruit juice in a small pan and heat gently to dissolve. Slowly stir into the cooled pudding. Pour into a rinsed 1½-pint (1-litre, 4-cup) mould and allow to set. When firm turn out and decorate with cream and angelica.

STRAWBERRY CREAM DESSERT

Cooking time 15 minutes
Serves 4

AMERICAN	IMPERIAL/METRIC
¼ cup tiny pasta rings	1 oz./25 g. tiny pasta rings
1 13½-oz. can strawberries	1 13½-oz./383-g. can strawberries
2 tablespoons cornstarch	½ oz./15 g. cornflour
1 5-oz. can evaporated milk	1 5-oz./142-g. can evaporated milk
6 tablespoons cold water	5 tablespoons cold water
1 tablespoon sugar	1 tablespoon sugar
2 teaspoons gelatin	2 teaspoons gelatine
½ cup coffee cream	scant ¼ pint/1 dl. single cream
whipped cream	whipped cream

Cook the pasta rings as previously directed until soft, drain, refresh with cold water and drain again.

Liquidise the strawberries or pass through a sieve. Make a blended sauce with the cornflour, evaporated milk, water and half the strawberry purée, add the sugar and remove from the heat. Soften the gelatine in 4 tablespoons of the purée, allow to stand for 2 minutes, then stir into the hot sauce. When the gelatine has dissolved add the remaining purée. Cool slightly, then stir in the cream and pasta. Turn into individual glasses and allow to set. Decorate with whipped cream.

PINEAPPLE CREAM SHELLS

Cooking time 15 minutes
Serves 4

AMERICAN	IMPERIAL/METRIC
¾ cup mini pasta shells or short cut macaroni	3 oz./75 g. mini pasta shells or short cut macaroni
1 medium can pineapple pieces	1 medium can pineapple pieces
1 large fresh lemon	1 large fresh lemon
1 large can condensed milk	1 large can condensed milk
candied cherries and candied angelica leaves	glacé cherries and angelica

Cook the pasta shells as previously directed. Drain and turn into a small soufflé dish. Drain the juice from the pineapple and reserve. Grate the rind from the lemon and squeeze out the juice. Arrange the pineapple over the pasta and pour over a little of the juice. Pour the condensed milk into a basin and gradually stir in 4 tablespoons of the fresh lemon juice together with the grated rind. When beginning to thicken stir in a little of the pineapple juice. Allow 2–3 minutes for the milk to thicken then spoon over the pudding. Decorate with cherries and angelica then chill, if possible, before serving.

Cooking time 10 minutes
Serves 4

AMERICAN	IMPERIAL/METRIC
$\frac{3}{4}$ cup pasta shells	3 oz./75 g. pasta shells
$1\frac{1}{4}$ cups whipping cream	$\frac{1}{2}$ pint/3 dl. double cream
1 egg white	1 egg white
1 1 lb. 13-oz. can apricots	1 1 lb. 13-oz./822-g. can apricots
$\frac{1}{4}$ cup sugar	2 oz./50 g. sugar

Cook the shells in boiling slightly salted water for 10 minutes, drain, rinse in cold water and allow to cool. Meanwhile whip the cream until thick and the egg white until fluffy. Drain the apricots and reserve four to decorate the top of the sweets. Make the remainder into a purée in a liquidiser or food mill. Then fold the shells into the cream and add the beaten egg white and sugar. In individual dessert glasses, layer apricot purée with cream mixture, ending with a layer of purée on top. Decorate each with a halved apricot.

Illustrated on page 64

Cooking time 20–25 minutes
Oven temperature 350°F., 180°C., Gas Mark 4
Serves 6

AMERICAN	IMPERIAL/METRIC
$\frac{1}{2}$ lb. egg vermicelli	8 oz./225 g. egg vermicelli
$\frac{1}{3}$ cup candied peel	2 oz./50 g. candied peel
$\frac{1}{2}$ cup almonds	2 oz./50 g. almonds
$\frac{1}{4}$ cup butter	2 oz./50 g. butter
$\frac{1}{3}$ cup seedless white raisins	2 oz./50 g. sultanas
$\frac{1}{4}$ teaspoon ground cinnamon	$\frac{1}{4}$ teaspoon ground cinnamon
$\frac{1}{4}$ cup granulated sugar	2 oz./50 g. castor sugar
2 eggs	2 eggs
$\frac{2}{3}$ cup whipping cream	$\frac{1}{4}$ pint/1$\frac{1}{2}$ dl. double cream

Cook the vermicelli as previously directed. Chop the peel, blanch the almonds and cut into slivers. Drain the vermicelli well, return to the pan, add the butter in small pieces and stir until melted. Add the sultanas and candied peel; stir in half the almonds. Mix the cinnamon with the sugar and stir in, add the beaten eggs and mix well. Turn the mixture into a buttered ovenproof dish. Scatter over the remaining almonds and bake for 10–15 minutes until set, then brown under a medium grill until crisp on top. Serve with cream.

Preparation time 10 minutes plus setting time
Serves 4

AMERICAN	IMPERIAL/METRIC
1 4-oz. package lemon-flavored gelatin	1 lemon jelly
$\frac{2}{3}$ cup boiling water	$\frac{1}{4}$ pint/1$\frac{1}{2}$ dl. boiling water
1 7-oz. can fruit cocktail	1 7-oz./198-g. can fruit cocktail
1 tablespoon cooked pasta alphabets	1 tablespoon cooked pasta alphabets
whipped cream for serving	whipped cream for serving

Dissolve the jelly in the boiling water, then add the juice from the can of fruit and make up to 1 pint (5$\frac{1}{2}$ dl., 2$\frac{1}{2}$ cups) with cold water. Add the fruit and cooked pasta. Rinse a mould with cold water. Pour in a layer of the stirred jelly and put into the freezing compartment of the fridge to set quickly. Stir the remaining jelly occasionally to prevent setting. When the jelly begins to firm pour on another layer and repeat until all the jelly is used. This prevents the pasta and fruit from sinking. Turn out when set.

BAKED MACARONI PUDDING

Cooking time about 1 hour
Oven temperature 350°F., 180°C., Gas Mark 4
Serves 4–6

AMERICAN	IMPERIAL/METRIC
¾ cup short cut macaroni	3 oz./75 g. short cut macaroni
2 tablespoons butter	1 oz./25 g. butter
2 tablespoons custard pudding mix	½ oz./15 g. custard powder
¼ cup sugar	2 oz./50 g. sugar
2½ cups creamy milk	1 pint/6 dl. creamy milk
½ teaspoon vanilla extract	½ teaspoon vanilla essence

Cook the macaroni as previously directed but for only 5 minutes; drain. Melt the butter and lightly butter an ovenproof dish. Turn the partly cooked macaroni into the dish. Blend the custard powder and sugar with a little of the milk and pour this, together with the remaining ingredients, into the dish and stir. Place in a moderate oven and cook for 1 hour, stirring occasionally.

SWEET NOODLES

Cooking time 35–40 minutes
Oven temperature 375°F., 190°C., Gas Mark 5
Serves 4

AMERICAN	IMPERIAL/METRIC
¼ lb. egg noodles	4 oz./100 g. egg noodles
2 tablespoons butter	1 oz./25 g. butter
3 tablespoons fine bread crumbs	2 tablespoons fine breadcrumbs
⅓ cup apricot jam	4 tablespoons apricot jam
1 cup ground walnuts	4 oz./100 g. ground walnuts
¼ cup sugar	2 oz./50 g. sugar
⅔ cup whipping cream	¼ pint/1½ dl. double cream

Cook the noodles as previously directed, drain well. Butter a soufflé dish and sprinkle with the breadcrumbs. Put layers of noodles, jam, noodles and ground walnuts mixed with sugar into the dish, starting and finishing with noodles. Cook in a moderately hot oven for 20–25 minutes. Turn out and serve hot with the cream.

CREAMY ORANGE MACARONI

Cooking time 30 minutes
Serves 4

AMERICAN	IMPERIAL/METRIC
1 cup short cut macaroni	4 oz./100 g. short cut macaroni
1 15-oz. can evaporated milk	1 15-oz./425-g. can evaporated milk
1 11-oz. can mandarin oranges	1 11-oz./312-g. can mandarin oranges
2 tablespoons butter	1 oz./25 g. butter
¼ cup soft brown sugar	2 oz./50 g. soft brown sugar
3 tablespoons concentrated orange drink	2 tablespoons orange squash
grated rind of 1 orange	grated rind of 1 orange

Cook the macaroni in a large pan as previously directed; drain. Return to the pan, together with the evaporated milk, ¼ pint (1½ dl., ⅔ cup) mandarin juice, butter and sugar. Stir well, cover and simmer gently for 10 minutes. Remove from the heat and allow to stand, still covered with a lid, for a further 10 minutes, then add the orange squash and grated orange rind. Turn into a serving dish and decorate with mandarin segments. Serve while still warm.

PASTA PARTIES

At party time pasta really comes into its own. Some of my most successful parties have centred round pasta, served sometimes for reasons of economy but mostly for fun. The whole atmosphere is gay and continental even in the middle of winter, with pasta and wine.

Nowadays catering for a party is expensive but if you really like to feed your guests then this is certainly an excellent and easy way to cope. All the dishes can be made in advance and simply heated at the right moment. Again the freezer is a great help in party catering but certainly not essential; however, if you have a friend or neighbour who has some spare freezer space make some sauces or lasagne in advance then you have all the last-minute time for the table and yourself. Summer parties are fun with pasta salads as these are easy to serve outside if the weather permits. The large 1- and 2-litre bottles of wine now available are excellent for this type of party (see also page 77).

MENU ONE

Pâté with French bread or toast

Chicken and spinach cannelloni
Crisp green salad with French dressing

Caramel oranges

Valpolicella and Soave

Chicken and Spinach Cannelloni

Cooking time about 50 minutes
Oven temperature 400°F., 200°C., Gas Mark 6
Serves 10–12

AMERICAN	IMPERIAL/METRIC
24 tubes cannelloni	24 tubes cannelloni
7½ cups tomato sauce (see page 12)	3 pints/1¾ litres tomato sauce (see page 12)
4 cups chopped cooked chicken	1½ lb./675 g. cooked chicken
½ cup butter	4 oz./100 g. butter
1½ lb. frozen chopped spinach	1½ lb./675 g. frozen chopped spinach
salt, pepper and nutmeg	salt, pepper and nutmeg
¼ cup grated Parmesan cheese	3 tablespoons grated Parmesan cheese
7½ cups béchamel sauce (see page 13)	3 pints/1¾ litres béchamel sauce (see page 13)

Cook the cannelloni until just tender, using two saucepans to prevent the cannelloni from sticking together when cooking. Drain, refresh with cold water, drain again, then lay out flat on a tray.

Prepare the tomato sauce. Mince or chop the chicken. Melt the butter and when hot stir in the spinach; cook until all the liquid has evaporated. Remove from the heat and stir in the minced or chopped chicken and seasonings. Add the tomato sauce and half the Parmesan cheese and mix well together. Divide the filling among the cooked cannelloni and roll up. Butter an ovenproof dish and arrange the cannelloni in it, with the joins on the underside. Cover with the béchamel sauce and dust over with cheese. Cover the top of the dish and reheat in a moderately hot oven for 20 minutes, then remove the lid and leave in the oven for a further 10 minutes to brown and crisp the top.

Fish scallops with white wine sauce served in scallop shells

Beef salad stroganoff
Green salad
Tomato salad
Mixed vegetable salad

Zabaglione

Cheese board with crackers

Chianti Classico

Beef Salad Stroganoff

Cooking time 30 minutes
Serves 12 party portions

AMERICAN	IMPERIAL/METRIC
3 lb. rump steak	3 lb./1¼ kg. rump steak
2 lb. Spanish onions	2 lb./900 g. Spanish onions
1 lb. button mushrooms	1 lb./450 g. button mushrooms
¼ cup oil	3 tablespoons oil
2 tablespoons butter	1 oz./25 g. butter
¾ cup flour	3 oz./75 g. flour
5 cups bouillon	2 pints/generous litre stock
½ cup tomato paste	5 oz./150 g. tomato purée
¼ cup lemon juice	3 tablespoons lemon juice
1 teaspoon Worcestershire sauce	1 teaspoon Worcestershire sauce
1 teaspoon French mustard	1 teaspoon French mustard
1 teaspoon horseradish sauce	1 teaspoon horseradish sauce
1 teaspoon onion salt	1 teaspoon onion salt
black pepper	black pepper
⅓ lb. egg noodles	6 oz./175 g. egg noodles
1 can red pimientos	1 can red pimentos
3 tablespoons chopped parsley	2 tablespoons chopped parsley
2 cups cultured sour cream	¾ pint/4 dl. soured cream

Cut the beef into thin strips about 3 inches (7½ cm.) long. Cut the onions into thin rings. Slice the mushrooms. Heat the oil and butter and add the beef a little at a time. Allow the meat to stiffen and colour. Remove each batch before sealing the remainder. Sauté the onions and mushrooms for 2–3 minutes. Add the flour and cook well. Gradually stir in the stock and tomato purée and bring to the boil, stirring. Return the meat to the pan together with the lemon juice and all the seasonings. Cover the pan and simmer gently for 12–15 minutes, until the beef is tender. Cook the noodles, drain, refresh with cold water and drain again. Allow the stroganoff to cool. Cut the pimento into thin strips, chop the parsley. Stir the noodles and soured cream into the stroganoff and then turn into a serving dish. Garnish with a criss-cross pattern of pimento and sprinkle with the parsley. Alternatively, the salad can be served hot, with hot buttered noodles handed separately. Increase the noodles to 1½ lb. (675 g.) if serving hot.

Smoked fish pâté

Pork in sweet and sour sauce
Noodles
Green beans or bean shoots
Mushrooms
Crisp green salad

Chocolate mousse

Bardolino red or dry Orvieto

Pork in Sweet and Sour Sauce

Cooking time 55 minutes
Serves 10–12

AMERICAN	IMPERIAL/METRIC
2½ lb. pork tenderloin	2½ lb./generous kg. pork fillet
good shake garlic salt	good shake garlic salt
3 tablespoons soy sauce	2 tablespoons soy sauce
oil for frying	oil for frying
	Sauce
1 12-oz. can pineapple pieces	1 12-oz./340-g. can pineapple pieces
4 carrots	4 carrots
4 green sweet peppers	4 green peppers
2½ cups chicken bouillon	1 pint/6 dl. chicken stock
½ cup brown sugar	6 tablespoons demerara sugar
⅔ cup soy sauce	8 tablespoons soy sauce
⅔ cup oil	8 tablespoons oil
⅔ cup vinegar	8 tablespoons vinegar
⅓ cup cornstarch	4 tablespoons cornflour
8 small dill pickled cucumbers	8 gherkins
¾ cup mustard pickle	4 oz./100 g. mustard pickle
good pinch ground ginger	good pinch ground ginger
1¾ lb. egg noodles or rings	1¾ lb./800 g. egg noodles or rings

Cut the pork fillets into small rings and flatten slightly with a rolling pin. Season with garlic salt and soy sauce. Sauté in hot oil for about 5 minutes on each side. This may have to be done in two batches. Remove and keep warm.

Drain the pineapple and reserve the juice. Cut the carrots and green peppers into thin strips; simmer in the pineapple juice and half the stock for 5 minutes. Mix the sugar, soy sauce, oil and vinegar together and add to the vegetables. Cook for a further 3 minutes. Thicken the sauce with the cornflour, blended with the remaining cold stock. Add the chopped gherkins, pineapple, mustard pickle and ginger.

Cook the egg noodles or rings as previously directed. Drain and arrange on a dish, making a border with the pasta. Arrange the pork fillet medallions in the centre and pour over the sweet and sour sauce.

Melon cocktail

Spaghetti bolognese

Cassata or ice cream
Lemon cheesecake

Chianti

Spaghetti with Bolognese Sauce

Cooking time 1 hour
Serves 10

AMERICAN	IMPERIAL/METRIC
6 slices bacon, chopped	6 rashers bacon, chopped
$\frac{1}{2}$ cup butter	4 oz./100 g. butter
4 medium-sized onions, finely chopped	4 medium-sized onions, finely chopped
1 clove garlic, crushed	1 clove garlic, crushed
4 small carrots, finely chopped	4 small carrots, finely chopped
4 stalks celery, finely chopped	4 stalks celery, finely chopped
2 cups lean ground beef	1 lb./450 g. lean minced beef
1 cup ground veal	8 oz./225 g. minced veal
1 cup ground pork	8 oz./225 g. minced pork
$1\frac{1}{4}$ cups chicken bouillon	$\frac{1}{2}$ pint/3 dl. chicken stock
$1\frac{1}{4}$ cups dry white wine	$\frac{1}{2}$ pint/3 dl. dry white wine
1 20-oz. can Italian plum tomatoes	1 20-oz./567-g. can Italian plum tomatoes
$\frac{1}{4}$ cup tomato paste	3 tablespoons tomato purée
$1\frac{1}{2}$ teaspoons salt	$1\frac{1}{2}$ teaspoons salt
freshly ground black pepper	freshly ground black pepper
1 clove	1 clove
good pinch freshly grated nutmeg	good pinch freshly grated nutmeg
3 cups sliced mushrooms	12 oz./350 g. mushrooms, sliced
6 chicken livers, chopped	6 chicken livers, chopped
$\frac{2}{3}$ cup whipping cream	8 tablespoons double cream
$2\frac{1}{2}$ lb. spaghetti	$2\frac{1}{2}$ lb./generous kg. spaghetti
$\frac{1}{4}$ cup butter	2 oz./50 g. butter
$\frac{1}{4}$ cup ripe olives (optional)	2 oz./50 g. black olives (optional)

In a frying pan, fry the chopped bacon in the butter, then add the onions and garlic and allow to cook for 2 minutes without browning. Add the carrots and celery and allow to cook gently for a few minutes. Set aside the vegetables in a saucepan and brown the beef, minced veal and pork in the frying pan. Add to the vegetables in the saucepan with the stock, wine, canned tomatoes, tomato purée, seasonings, spices, mushrooms and chicken livers.
Allow to simmer gently for 45 minutes to 1 hour. Stir in the cream just before serving the sauce with the cooked spaghetti which has been tossed in melted butter. Hand grated Parmesan cheese separately. A garnish of black olives is tasty if you like them.

Illustrated on page 20 and the jacket

Italy stretches from the Alps to the Mediterranean and offers a huge variety of climates and soils. Different types of wine are produced by different climatic conditions and soil and Italy has her own grape varieties and traditions of wine making and is in fact the world's largest wine producer. From the viewpoint of quality and price Italian wines are highly competitive.

In 1963 Italy passed a law giving nationally enforceable protection to the names of wines. Already there are over 140 approved wines, guaranteed to be of 'particular reputation and worth', which bear on their bottles the words DOC (Denominazione de Origine Controllata). This means that the wine is from the area named, produced from the laid-down proportions of specific grapes by the traditional methods. The vintage year on the bottle must be accurate and the wine properly aged. The vineyards have been carefully surveyed and each has a maximum production and yield which cannot be exceeded. Lesser wines are marked with the words 'Simple Denomination'.

The map indicates the different wines available to us and the areas they come from and as it would take more space than I have left to go over all of them, I think it is more helpful to know what the label on your bottle means.

The name The name of the wine is usually geographical as you can see by the map, e.g., *Chianti* (large area) or *Valpolicella* (a district). However, the name can indicate a grape variety used, e.g., *Barbera* or *Verdicchio*. A common grape is often further defined by a place name, e.g., *Barbera d'Alba*. A few purely historical names are used such as *Est Est Est* which has rather a nice story. In the twelfth century a German bishop was travelling to Rome and he sent his steward ahead to find inns with good wine. He was to mark the inn by chalking *Est* on the door. At Montefiascone his enthusiasm was such that he chalked *Est Est Est*.

The producer's name This is sometimes the name and the town but often prefixed with *Produttori* (producer), *Cantine* (cellars), *Cantina Sociale* (co-operative producer), *Casa Vinicola* (wine house), *Tenuta* (estate).

DOC I have already explained this term as the national guarantee of genuineness, to be found on the main label over or under the wine name.

Vintages This is on the main label or a shoulder label – *Annata* (year), *Vendemmia* (vintage).

Grower's Consortia Seals The seal label of a Consortium still appears as a sign of careful control, on paper usually at the top of the neck, across the edge of the foil cork cover. There may be a bottle number which indicates limited production.

Bottling This usually takes place in or near the production area and is indicated by producers, e.g., *Imbottigliato* (bottled) or *Infiascato* (put in flasks), *in zona d'origine* (in the growing area) or *nello stabilimento* (at the producer's premises).

Description Words such as *Extra, Fine, Selezionato* are forbidden by law. Under DOC regulations, *Vecchio* (old) and *Riserva* (reserve) guarantee ageing.

Classico This is used after the wine name, e.g., *Valpolicella Classico*, and means that the wine comes from the heart of a particular production area.

Lombardy
Valtellina, Frecciarossa, Clastidio, Chiaretto del Garda

Piedmont
Barolo, Barbaresco, Gattinara, Barbera, Asti Spumante

Liguria
Cinqueterre

Tuscany
Chianti Classico, Colli Aretini, Colli Fiorentini, Colline Pisane, Colli Senesi, Montalbano, Rufina, Brunello di Montalcino

Umbria
Orvieto, Torgiano

Latium
Frascati (Castelli Romani), Est Est Est di Montefiascone, Aprilia

Sardinia
Vernaccia, Cannonau, Torbato

Campania
Ischia, Ravello, Lacrima Christi

Sicily
Etna, Corvo, Faro, Capo

Trentino Alto-Adige
Teroldego, Casteller, Lago di Caldaro, Terlaner, Pinot, Merlot, Traminer

Friuli-Venezia Giulia
Pinot, Cabernet, Tocai, Riesling

Veneto
Valpolicella, Bardolino, Soave, Recioto, Prosecco di Conegliano, Cabernet, Merlot

Emilia-Romagna
Lambrusco, Sangiovese, Albana

The Marches
Verdicchio dei Castelli di Iesi, Verdicchio di Matelica, Rosso Conero, Rosso Piceno

Abruzzo and Molise
Montepulciano, Trebbiano

Apulia
Castel del Monte, San Severo, Locorontondo

Basilicata
Aglianico del Vulture

Calabria
Ciro

PASTA IN YOUR FREEZER

Pasta is no longer a strange word in this country and as we mix more freely with our neighbours in the Common Market it will surely figure more and more in our everyday menus. Spaghetti, macaroni, rings, alphabets and noodles have become everyday ingredients in many of the convenience foods on sale today. Now, with the increasing appetites of freezer owners, we can buy the specialities of our favourite Italian restaurants as lasagne verdi and cannelloni take their place in the freezer counters with the steak and kidney pies. However, these speciality dishes are still expensive from the freezer counters so why not freeze your own. The adventurous freezer cook will want to experiment with her own pasta dishes for the freezer. It is a great advantage to freeze sauces to serve with pasta but it is also possible to freeze composite dishes which are useful for individual portions or using up leftovers.

TO FREEZE PLAIN PASTA

1   Use only good quality hard pasta with a protein content of at least 12%. You will need $2\frac{1}{2}$–3 oz. (60–75 g.) uncooked dried pasta per person.

2   Cook the pasta in the usual way in boiling, salted water until firm. If you know the pasta is being cooked for the freezer undercook by about 2 minutes. Rinse the pasta with cold water immediately it is cooked as this prevents the pasta continuing to cook in its own heat.

3   To stop the pasta sticking together stir in sufficient oil with a wooden fork, try not to mash the pasta while doing so.

4   Pack in plastic or foil containers with a lid.

TO USE FROM THE FREEZER

1   Tip into plenty of boiling, salted water, i.e., 10 oz. (275 g.) pasta will need 2 pints (generous litre, 5 cups) water.

2   Only allow the water enough time to return to the boil or you will overcook the pasta.

As previously mentioned, sauces, e.g., bolognese or milanese, can be cooked in large quantities and frozen in portions suitable for your own needs. I usually freeze in portions of two, four and six servings either in plastic boxes, polythene bags or aluminium foil bags.

TO FREEZE COMPOSITE DISHES

1   Place the pasta in the middle of the container with the sauce around the *outside*, and cover with a lid.

2   To reheat place the dish or foil container in the oven with the lid in place. Although this seems strange you will find the pasta reheats more quickly than the sauce and this method prevents the pasta overcooking and sticking whilst the sauce is heating. The moisture from the sauce will keep the pasta in good condition during reheating. Layered dishes such as lasagne may be cooked without a lid providing there is a generous layer of sauce and cheese on top. Cover dishes such as cannelloni with foil and finish under the grill if sprinkled with grated cheese.

Individual portions are more difficult to freeze; however, if a foil container or small dish is used place the pasta diagonally across the dish and the sauce in the other half of the square or rectangle. Reheat with a lid and the sauce will spread a little keeping the pasta moist.

INDEX